THE GOOD LIFE EATERY COOKBOOK

1 3 5 7 9 10 8 6 4 2

Ebury Press, an imprint of Ebury Publishing,
20 Vauxhall Bridge Road,
London, SW1V 2SA

Ebury Press is part of the Penguin Random House group of companies whose addresses
can be found at global.penguinrandomhouse.com

Penguin
Random House
UK

Text © Shirin Kouros and Yasmine Larizadeh 2016
Photography by Toby Glanville

First published by Ebury Press in 2016

www.penguin.co.uk

A CIP catalogue record for this book is available from the British Library

Project editor: Louise McKeever
Design: Two Associates
Photography: Toby Glanville
Illustrations: Marco Zamora
Food stylist: Frankie Unsworth
Prop stylist: Jo Harris
Production: Helen Everson

ISBN: 9781785031571

Colour origination by Altaimage, London
Printed and bound in Italy by Printer Trento

Penguin Random House is committed to a sustainable future for
our business, our readers and our planet. This book is made from
Forest Stewardship Council® certified paper.

MIX
Paper from
responsible sources
FSC® C018179

THE GOOD LIFE EATERY COOKBOOK

SHIRIN KOUROS AND YASMINE LARIZADEH

EBURY PRESS

CONTENTS

INTRODUCTION

WHO WE ARE

We are Central London's first fast, casual, health-orientated eatery and cold-pressed juice bar. Opening our doors to the general public back in August 2013, we are now three locations strong and CANNOT WAIT to share our amazing recipes, stories and philosophies with you – mainly to explain to you why we are so OBSSESED with FOOD. (It's a healthy obsession, WE PROMISE.)

We are more than just an eatery; we are a part of your everyday lives. We strive to encourage everyone to eat better, healthier and become happier as a result. Our love for food and cooking was borne from the way we were raised. This not only came from our Iranian background and cultural standpoint, but also our general approach to eating fresh produce and eating well.

We are not diet food fanatics. We are not boring and we definitely won't encourage you to eat anything unless it looks and tastes like a million bucks! I've always found it difficult to reason with people who think food should not be a pleasure but just a form of sustenance... And what is our response? We are here to prove all those people wrong! We create good old-fashioned, QUALITY, freshly made food that just so happens to be good for you.

DON'T OVERCOMPLICATE IT.
KEEP IT SIMPLE. KEEP IT CLEAN. KEEP IT FRESH.

Why would you even bother overcomplicating your life? Simplicity is the key! Using straightforward ingredients in their simplest form is the way to go, especially since we don't always know what some of the ingredients in supermarket products are.

WE ARE FOR EVERYONE!

Boys, girls, mums, dads, grandpas, grandmas, vegans, vegetarians; if you're gluten-free, if you're dairy-free, even if you're all of the above – WE CATER TO ALL!

OUR BACKGROUND

We both have a strong sense of belonging when it comes to our Iranian heritage, and Shirin and I hope you can identify this ingrained inspiration throughout our recipes – from the ingredients we use to some of the methods we turn to. Mealtimes have always been highly respected within our communities and it is how we as families come together.

Our everyday lives now revolve around food, due to our current occupations – so much so that we feel like you can almost lose your sense of importance when it comes to mealtimes. Always reminding ourselves about where we are from brings us back to the initial realisation of what mealtimes, apart from feeding oneself, actually consist of – socialising, reflection, relaxation and just general downtime.

We are so lucky and so very fortunate to be able to say that there was never a moment that went by in which we were hungry or underfed or unhappy about the relationship we have with food. Our parents and grandparents showed us how to have respect and appreciation towards real food and unfortunately not many people are able to or decide to manifest this today.

Iranian cooking practices are against cutting corners. We feel as if the majority of philosophies these days tend to enforce the contrary, in relation to the demands of the fast-paced world we live in. This is an attitude that we live by at The Good Life and, in fact, place the utmost importance on; when you start cutting corners, you start losing the love, the respect and real grassroots appreciation towards what we eat.

THE FIVE SENSES

We believe that food should be a sensory experience and we consider this another fundamental principle of cooking that has come all the way from the Persian Empire – from the scents of the vast spice markets to going out and foraging, hunting or fishing for your food. It is important to see, feel, smell, taste and even hear the various stages of nourishing oneself, from acquiring your ingredients to cooking them, and to putting the finished food in your mouth.

I remember when I was younger I would visit my grandmother in north Iran where she would prepare some of the most mouthwatering, delicious meals I have ever eaten in my whole life. The meals always started with going to the market and seeing live animals being slaughtered right in front of you – gruesome, I know. I remember when I was six years old I actually took a goose (aka Goosey) home because I couldn't bear the thought of having to eat him later on that evening for dinner. After buying the animal from the market, it was then plucked and butchered. The fruit and veg which would accompany the meat were picked from my grandmother's allotments and orchards. We rarely see this any more, and our perception of meat, fish, poultry, fruits and veg is usually conveyed as a cleanly cut item sitting in a plastic package on a supermarket shelf... no personal feeling or work goes into the preparation any more and we are often disconnected from our food.

Funnily and coincidentally enough, when we opened our first café location on Sloane Avenue in London so many people started asking us if we had named the café after *The Good Life* show on the BBC, and our response was pretty much 'Ummm no, don't really know what that is, but it's a great Kanye West and Inner City song…' (Now we know the show was quite before our time and I only moved to the UK when I was nine ANNNNDDD we love music.) So after the seventh person mentioned it, I was rather curious and went onto our trusty friend Google to see what all the fuss was about… TOTALLY GENIUS and TOTALLY RELATIVE. For those of you who don't know, it was aired in the 1970s and is considered one of Britain's greatest comedy sitcoms. It portrayed the life of a couple who escape London's modern commercial living and move out to the countryside to lead a totally self-sufficient life by converting their garden into a farm and growing their own crops. Funny how that worked out, huh?

CALI LIVIN'

Shirin and I were both born in the USA, so as well as our Iranian heritage, the forward-thinking, innovative nation that is THE UNITED STATES OF 'MURICA needs to get a bit of street credit ova here. Being exposed to such foodie wonders in Los Angeles and New York City from a very young age opened up our taste buds to a whole new vision of food and eating. Nearly every street corner in the city of Los Angeles has some kind of healthy offering – they don't even need to mention the words 'health' as it is fundamentally a given there, just SIMPLE, REAL FOOD. This led us onto our supreme curiosity as to why it hadn't really been done over here in the UK back in 2012. And more specifically, why was healthy food nearly always related to extreme diets and weird 'foods' that weren't at all natural? Why not wait for a quick hot minute to consume something that has been made especially for you, tailored to your every whim and want? Rather than something so uniformly ubiquitous that you just grab it off a shelf and then herd over to the till to pay for it.

WHERE IT ALL BEGAN

In January 2013, I, Yasmine Larizadeh, an American-born, ethnically Iranian, British Citizen, met Shirin Kourous, an American-born, half Iranian/half Swiss (talk about not complicating things, hey?) who had only just recently moved to London. After complaining to our parents all day about the empty, unfulfilled, vacant lives we were living, I guess they finally realised that together we would be a good (?) fit. Ha ha ha ha.

We met one brisk winter's day at Shirin's flat after coming back from our Christmas holidays to discuss our shared interest in simple, healthy, fresh food and whether or not we could endeavour to bring something new to London's food scene. We both came to the same conclusion – there was a massive gap in the market for a healthy, good-for-you eatery, as no one wants to eat starchy white bread any more… ENOUGH OF THIS MADNESS. It was pretty much ready, steady, GO from there onwards. Following a year-and-a-half long research and development programme, beginning in Los Angeles and ending in London with a rigorous restaurant training scheme, we embarked on finding a site, and after several disagreements, laughs, cries, general mixed feelings and emotions THE GOOD LIFE EATERY CAME TO LIFE.

LIVIN' THE LIFE OF A START-UP

We really have lived it here at The Good Life Eatery. It's all well and good to run a successful business, but there will always be some sort of shortfall, especially when you're just starting up. I'm looking back on this crazy journey that we have come on, and a very deep breath is in order.

We started with close to no previous experience in running a restaurant. In hindsight, it probably wasn't the best of ideas. I'm surprised no one told us not to do it, but I guess you need to surround yourself with people who will encourage you in these situations – or have no idea! Ha ha ha. Nevertheless, it was one of those things where you just kind of had to rip off the plaster and go for it. Learning by doing is the key to running a successful business – and I don't mean telling someone else to do it. I genuinely mean from washing the dishes, to cooking in the kitchen, to making the coffees, to locking up at the end of the day.

Finding a site was probably the most challenging hurdle to get over. In the UK your covenance seems to be the most important thing when it comes to approaching landlords, but obviously, in our case, we had none. We were a newly founded company with zero track record. Unfortunately some commercial institutions and governmental organisations tend to over-promise things that they can't usually deliver on, mainly in regards to helping small businesses establish themselves and/or grow, nevertheless, we managed to find one person who actually believed in us to give us some backing (which is key for a start-up – shout out to our boys in Saudi!).

After nearly six months of knocking on doors, we finally managed to acquire a site, albeit with an extremely hefty rent deposit. After signing the daunting commitment of a ten-year lease, it was literally then a scene from an *Oliver Twist* movie – begging, borrowing, (no stealing). The chairs in our store were discarded from an upscale restaurant in Central London, which I'm nearly 100 per cent sure my joiner found in a skip on the side of the road. The entire bar area and shelving was made out of reclaimed scaffolding boards and poles... oh, and we found the lamps, which are currently hanging over the bar in our friend's garage, and are still on loan... (Message to the K boys – WE ARE KEEPING THEM AND WE LOVE YOU).

It hasn't been easy, but I can actually say with not a single shadow of a doubt, it has all been worth it. I don't think anything (from working nearly 20 hours a day to using my car as a storage unit – don't ask) will ever come close to getting in the way of the wisdom, love and fulfillment we have experienced over the last few years.

LOCAL OVER ORGANIC

We firmly believe local produce is the most beneficial when you are looking at the future big picture. The ideal choice would be local AND organic but usually that is not very accessible due to a variety of contributing factors. The majority of local farmers we have encountered in and around the UK do practise organic processes but find it very difficult to receive the seal of approval and certifications due to costs and the mountains of laborious paperwork involved. We buy fresh seasonal produce as much as we possibly can and try our utmost to reflect this through our outlets across London.

Now, we're not saying go and scour the streets or totally change every ingredient of a recipe to fit the profile of something that has been grown around the corner from where you're preparing it, but always consider it when hitting up your local. If you do find a local farmers' market, go see what's up and what's currently on offer and in season. There are also lots of local products available in most major supermarkets and grocery shops, it just takes that little bit of extra time to browse. This not only gives mad inspiration for later cooking seshs, but I definitely think it opens your eyes to a bit more information and grasp on what we are currently eating.

We have tried our best to let you know which recipes can be tweaked to keep it local, seasonal and FRAICHHHHEEEE. I do urge you all to give it a go; ASK QUESTIONS, PUSH BOUNDARIES AND KEEP CURIOUS, PEOPLEZZZZZ.

GET YOUR PREP ONNNNNN

Sunday nights are for preppinnnnnn' for the week (not just for Sundays), especially for someone like me who is: a) the world's biggest procrastinator; and b) rather lazy in nature. There's a reason why we do prep at restaurants, otherwise we wouldn't be able to get all those amazingly yummy dishes out in a timely fashion. We suggest you live by this at home as it cuts down the prep on the day and cooking time. It also helps with enhancing flavours, in relation to marinating, which we LOVEEEEEEE. Just trust me on this one, it will help to organise your life and aid the incorporation of a well-balanced diet. Also it is less messy if you're peeling and chopping the previous night, CAMAAANNNNNNN.

OUR EATERIES

We currently have three Café locations in Central London, with hopes of expanding organically over the coming years. Our aim is to make our concept and the notion of healthy eating more accessible to all scopes of demographics.

The cafés are all around the same size, with similar layouts, ranging from 30–35 seats for eating-in. We provide both take-away and delivery services within a mile radius of each location, and some of our products are available to purchase online. For the interior of each spot we have made a point of using as many sustainable materials as possible. The nature and breathability of certain organic materials are key to creating an air of warmth, especially in the dead of England's blustery winters, and let's be honest now, PEEPS, it looks AWESOME!

We don't have Wifi, which has been an ongoing battle with our customers over the years, but we're going to stick to our guns on this one. It was a moving moment when one crisp, autumn day I walked in to check on the morning service and there was an entire row of customers either reading the newspaper or speaking to one another...

Strangely enough, I was sitting next to one of our most loyal customers in the Chelsea branch not so long ago and she started telling me the reason why she loves coming to us is because she feels comfortable. Alone, on a date with her husband, or with friends, she has always felt welcome and part of something. This was a clear moment in my mind when I thought to myself, WE DID IT!

Our staff; I don't even know where to begin apart from mentioning that we couldn't have done any of this without you all. The amount of support has been overwhelming and we have gained so much knowledge and inspiration from each and every one of you (getting all teary eyed ova hereeeee). We have tried our utmost to provide an exceptional level of service and guidance when it comes to interacting with our customers and we hope that each and every one of you using our book will have the chance to come by and say HEeeEeeEyYYyyYYY!!

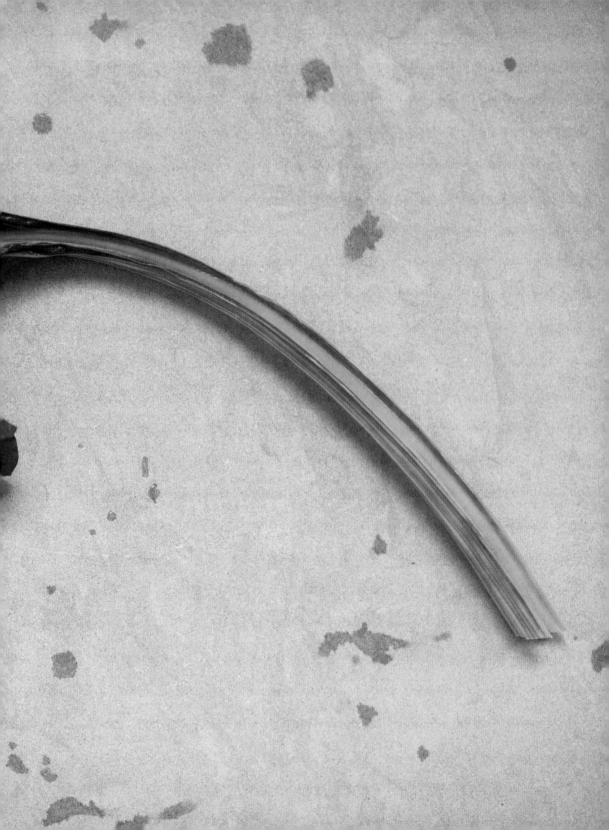

GLOSSARY

Acai berries/acai purée: The acai berry is a wondrous, reddish-purple, grape-like fruit that comes from the acai palm tree, native to Central and South America. Up until recent years it was a wild harvest, but with its growing popularity farming has started. The acai fruit pulp is considered to be even richer in antioxidants than cranberries, raspberries, blackberries, strawberries or blueberries. Acai berries do not travel well, therefore most of the time you will find it in pill, powder or frozen pulp form. We prefer the frozen pulp as you are also getting more fibre and it tastes DELISH in smoothies!

Agave nectar: The agave plant grows from the southwestern US through to the northern part of South America. It is actually the same plant that is used to make tequila. Agave gained popularity as it is lower on the glycemic index, but just like any natural sweetener, such as maple syrup or honey, it should be used sparingly.

Arrowroot powder: Arrowroot is an easily digested starch extracted from the roots of the arrowroot plant, native to South America. Arrowroot is a root starch that acts as a thickener, similar to cornstarch. Unlike cornstarch, which is a highly processed GMO, arrowroot is extracted in a fairly easy and natural way. It is quite simple to work with; you mix the arrowroot with an equal amount of cold water, and then whisk to a slurry. Add the slurry mixture into your sauce and you will immediately see it thicken up. It is best used at the end of cooking as it can break down in long, high-heat cooking. It has no flavour and it leaves sauces glossy and silky.

Barberries: I love using ingredients that bring me back to my roots, and these little red jewels know as barberries are incredibly useful things to have in the store cupboard – sprinkle them onto a dish of rice or couscous or strew over pot-roasted chicken, and they'll bring a burst of gorgeous colour and an explosion of tart flavour. They are often dried, as they don't keep well fresh. Just a random fact, Iranians use barberries as a key ingredient in certain wedding dishes, where their sourness stands as a symbol of the fact that life isn't always a bed of roses! You can find them in most Middle Eastern grocery stores or on Amazon, but make sure they are fresh. They are about half the size of a raisin and more tart than a cranberry. You know they are fresh when they are bright red; if they are brown in colour that means they have oxidised or are old. Make sure to wash and pick through the barberries as you sometimes find stones in the packet.

Bee pollen: Bee pollen is made by hard-working honeybees and is the main food of these bees. Bee pollen is now available commercially as a food supplement, meant to promote vitality. It is a tiny yellow pellet with a sweet flavour typically sprinkled on granola, yogurt, smoothies or porridge.

Buckwheat groats: DON'T LET THE NAME DECEIVE YOU! Buckwheat is not wheat, nor is it related to wheat in any way, it is actually derived from the seeds of a flowering plant. Therefore, like quinoa, it is naturally gluten-free. It can be baked into granolas, like our recipe on page 29, but buckwheat is also a good binding agent. When soaked, it becomes very gelatinous and can be used in baking.

Cacao nibs: Cacao nibs are simply unprocessed cacao beans broken into little pieces. These little dark nibs are great sprinkled on your morning porridge or smoothie, stirred into any cookies or baked goods and also nice just to munch on alone. They are also rich in magnesium.

Chestnut flour: Chestnut flour is made from finely milled chestnuts. It is a beautiful flour to work with for gluten-free and paleo baking, but as it is quite pricey it also works well when combined with other, cheaper flours. It gives a nutty flavour to baked goods while also providing a great source of protein and fibre.

Chia seeds: These are tiny black seeds, slightly larger and similar in colour to poppy seeds. They come from a plant called *Salvia hispanica* from the mint family, native to central and southern Mexico and Guatemala. They are known for their ability to provide slow-release energy, and were once a staple food for the Aztecs and Mayans. These tiny seeds are a great way to boost the fibre, protein, calcium, antioxidants and omega-3s in your diet. In order to gain their full benefit, chia seeds should be soaked for about 20 minutes in double the amount of water until they swell and become gelatinous prior to consuming.

Chipotle in adobo sauce: This Mexican favourite really packs a punch. Chipotles are smoked and dried jalapeño peppers. Their flavour really comes out when they are marinated in adobo, a tangy, rich smoky sauce. OOOOO WEEEEE, give me some of that chilli!

Coconut cream: Is essentially coconut milk but much thicker. It is made in the same way as coconut milk, whereby the coconut flesh is grated and soaked in hot water and then drained. The cream is the thick, non-liquid part that seperates from coconut milk and rises to the top. It's great used in desserts and non-dairy mousses/creams.

Coconut flour: Is dried, pulverised, defatted coconut flesh. It is made from the coconut solids that are left over after the meat has been used to produce coconut milk. Coconut flour is not easily substituted for other gluten-free flours in recipes as it absorbs tremendous amounts of liquid.

Coconut oil: We are big fans of coconut oil at The Good Life Eatery. Not only is it full of the best kinds of saturated fat, but also holds up well under the heat of cooking, making it safe to fry and grill with. Coconut oil is the oil derived from the fatty flesh of coconuts. Try to reach for unrefined coconut oil; virgin and extra-virgin are both great, as it means they are made from the first pressings of raw virgin coconuts without any added chemicals.

Coconut, shredded: Is simply shredded and dried coconut flesh. Try to buy one with no added sweeteners or additives.

Dried sour lemons: Also known as 'Limoo Amani', these dried limes originated in the Persian Gulf and are very popular in Persian cuisine. They are left to dry in the sun to reduce their water content and are therefore dark brown and very hard. They are used whole, sliced or ground to give a tangy, sour and slightly bitter flavour to dishes. Whole dried lemons are often cooked in Iranian stews where they soften up so you can then pierce and eat them. You can find them on Amazon or in most Middle Eastern food shops.

Edamame beans: Edamame is a young soya bean that has been harvested before the beans have had a chance to harden. We mainly see them in their pods in Japanese restaurants, served lightly steamed with a sprinkling of sea salt. You can buy them shelled or in the pod, and usually frozen.

Farro: Farro is the term used for a group of three wheat species. In Italian cuisine, farro is distinguished in different sizes: *farro piccolo* (also known as einkorn), *farro medio* (also known as emmer), and *farro grande* (also known as spelt). The imported Italian farro available in the UK is usually the emmer variety. It is most often semi-pearled, meaning it retains some but not all of its bran and nutrients. This type of farro doesn't require soaking and defies the myth that it takes ages to cook, as it is ready in just 25 minutes.

Gluten-free flour: All-purpose gluten-free flour can be used as a substite for normal flour, but not exactly like for like. It is usually a blend of various flours that balance together to deliver a lightweight gluten-free baked good. We tend to use Bobs Red Mill or Doves Farm.

Goji berries: Goji berries, traditionally known as wolfberries, are the fruit of a plant. It's a bright orange-red berry similar to the size of a raisin but longer and harder and commonly grown in the north-central and western areas of China. The fresh ripe berry is easily damaged and does not travel well, therefore it's very unlikely to find fresh berries for purchase. They are most commonly found dry. We suggest soaking them in warm water to soften them up before sprinkling on your morning cereal or porridge. They are also a great addition to smoothies and granola.

Greens powder: A good-quality greens powder is like a multi-vitamin on steroids. The ingredients list is usually long and impressive and includes additions such as wheatgrass, spinach, kale and broccoli; algaes such as kelp, spirulina and chlorella, and probiotics and enzymes.

Harissa paste: Harisssa paste is a spicy aromatic paste made from chilli and an assortment of other spices and herbs. It is widely used in North African and Middle Eastern cuisines as a condiment, or mixed into stews, soups, couscous or other grains for added flavour. As it is strong and pungent, a little goes a long way. You can find it ready-made in jars and cans, and sometimes as a paste, in a tube. It is also available as a powder, to which you need to add fresh olive oil and garlic to use.

Hemp seeds: Hemp seeds come from the same hemp plant used to make durable materials such as clothing as well as – well, I am sure you know what else! The traditional hemp seeds that we use in our book are hulled. They are light beige in colour with a hint of green. They are nutty in flavour, perhaps best comparable to pine nuts, though of course the texture is quite different. Hemp seeds are a great source of protein, dietary fibre and good fats and can be eaten raw, ground into a meal, sprouted, made into hemp milk or simply sprinkled over a salad, granola or smoothie.

Linseed (flaxseeds): Golden linseeds, also known as flaxseeds, are powerhouses of nutrition. They have a subtle, nutty, slightly earthy flavour and are a relatively inexpensive superfood. They are available whole or ground, the latter is better for absorption. They are a rich source of omega 3 fats. If you are having them whole, the best way to get maximum nutrition is to soak them first. Put one heaped spoonful of seeds into a glass, cover with water and leave overnight. Add the swollen seeds and water to a smoothie or to your morning cereal, yogurt, acai bowl or porridge. Ground linseeds can be sprinkled directly onto your food or into your smoothie.

Matcha powder: Matcha literally means 'powdered tea'. Matcha is a finely milled, vibrant, green tea powder made from the highest quality Japanese green tea leaves. People often don't understand the difference between traditional green tea and matcha green tea. When you order traditional green tea, components from the leaves get infused into the hot water, and then the leaves are discarded, just like other loose-leaf teas. With matcha, you're drinking the entire leaf, which is made into a solution by mixing about a teaspoon of matcha powder with a third of a cup of hot but not boiling water, which is then whisked with a bamboo brush until it froths. Matcha tea is high in caffeine, even more so than coffee.

Maca powder: Maca, a root that belongs to the radish family, is commercially purchased as a beige powdery substance. Grown in the mountains of Peru, it has been called 'Peruvian ginseng'. Its flavour has been described as 'malted' or 'caramel like' and tastes best in smoothies, cakes, baked goods and raw desserts.

Miso paste: Miso is made from soya beans that have been fermented and turned into a paste. There are 4 main varieties of miso paste: white, yellow, red and black. Each variety has different ingredients added to the soya beans during fermentation, such as rice, barley, buckwheat and other grains that changes their flavour and colour. Miso has a very complex flavour and ability to add an extra heartiness or 'umami' to nearly any dish. Use it to marinate fish and other proteins or add to salad dressings and dips.

Nori seaweed: Nori seaweed basically looks like seaweed paper. Edible seaweed is shredded and then pressed into thin sheets. You can use it to make homemade sushi, crumble it on top of an Asian-inspired salad, stir-fry or lightly toast it in the oven with a drizzle of oil and salt for a savoury snack. You can find packages of it at any Asian grocery store, health food store and more and more frequently these days in your local supermarket.

Nut and seed milks: Are simply non-dairy-containing milks made out of filtered water, the nut or seed of your choice and any possible flavour additions. If you are avoiding dairy, nut and seed milks mean you can still have the same pleasure of an amazing bowl of granola. Nut milks are easy to make yourself or you can find them readily available in most supermarkets.

Nutritional yeast flakes: Nutritional yeast used to be known as that mysterious yellow fish-food-like flakes that only vegans used to give their food that cheesy flavour. Today we are seeing more and more of it sprinkled in salads and burgers as its nutty, cheesy taste really does give an extra kick of flavour. It's not the same as active yeast; so don't get fooled by the word yeast. Sprinkle it on popcorn, stir it into a veggie mash or add a little to the cooking water for 'cheesy grits' polenta or risotto, sprinkle on any pasta dish or make 'almond parmesan' by blending nutritional yeast with raw blanched almonds in a food processor.

Palm hearts: Hearts of palm are the edible cores from various palm tree species. They are firm and smooth and described as resembling the flavour of an artichoke heart. Finding fresh heart of palm is rare and expensive and they are most often found in cans or glass jars – I always go for glass jars when I can!

Piquillo peppers: The name piquillo means 'little beak' and that's exactly what they look like. Traditionally piquillo peppers are picked then roasted over open fires, peeled and then packed in jars or tins. They are sweet, spicy and smoky.

Protein powder: The most obvious reason to supplement with protein powder is to reach your protein intake goal for the day. However, they aren't absolutely needed if you can meet your protein needs with whole foods. Protein powder comes in various forms, such as whey, casein, soy, pea, brown rice and hemp, amongst others. Always choose a protein powder with few ingredients and without added chemicals.

Quinoa and quinoa flakes: Quinoa is a tiny bead-shaped seed with a slightly bitter flavour and firm texture. It may not be a household name just yet, but it is really getting there. This power seed was the staple crop to the Incas, growing high up in the Andes mountain range. Unlike wheat or rice, quinoa is a complete protein – containing all eight of the essential amino acids. It is an excellent source of plant-based protein, packed with dietary fibre, phosphorus, magnesium and iron. It

is naturally gluten-free and easy to digest. Quinoa flakes are simply made from pressed quinoa. Quinoa also comes in other varieties now, such as quinoa milk and popped quinoa.

Raw cacao powder: Raw cacao is the unrefined, unprocessed version of the cocoa powder you find at your local supermarket and it is made by cold-pressing unroasted cocoa beans. Raw cacao is available in most health food shops or online and is pricier than cocoa powder but you need much less. Cocoa and raw cacao can be used interchangeably in all our recipes, however, you will need almost twice the amount of cocoa powder to achieve the same result as the flavour is much weaker.

Spirulina: Spirulina is a microalgae that grows naturally in the wild, in warm, freshwater lakes, natural springs and saltwater. It is most often found in powder or tablet form. It has a deep blue-green colour which gives anything that it is mixed with a deep greenish hue. Spirulina contains a wide range of vitamins and minerals and it is easiest to consume when mixed into smoothies, yogurt or breakfast cereals.

Sumac: Native to the Middle East, the sumac bush produces deep red berries which are dried and ground into a coarse powder. Ground sumac has a tangy, lemony flavour, but more aromatic and less tart than lemon juice. It's used in everything from dry rubs, marinades and dressing but is best used sprinkled over food like cooked vegetables or meats before serving.

Tahini: Tahini, simply put, is sesame seed paste. It is a staple of Middle Eastern and Mediterranean cooking. It is most commonly known as a key ingredient in making hummus, however, its uses go far beyond that. It has a delicate roasted sesame flavour, without the sweetness that is common to many nut and seed butters. It's a great spread alternative for those with nut allergies, as it is a seed.

Tamari: Is a Japanese form of soy sauce and is made with no or very little wheat, while traditional soy sauce does contain wheat. Tamari has a darker colour and richer flavour than the common Chinese soy sauce you buy off the supermarket shelf. It also tastes more balanced and mild and less salty than the sometimes sharp bite of soy sauce, which makes it great for dipping. If you are avoiding gluten, double check that the tamari you are buying does not contain wheat.

Tofu: Tofu is basically a white block that is made by coagulating soya milk and then pressing the resulting curds into softish white blocks. It is a great source of protein, particularly for vegetarians and vegans, and the subtle taste allows it to absorb the flavour of whatever it is marinated and cooked in. Tofu comes in many different varieties, mainly soft, firm or extra firm. Try to avoid buying GMO tofu if you can.

Vanilla bean paste: Vanilla bean paste is essentially a small jar of the scraped-out vanilla pod. It is a great way to get the super-fragrant, sweet, speckled end product that you would achieve from a vanilla pod with the convenience of a quick scoop of the teaspoon.

Vanilla extract: Macerating vanilla beans in a mixture of alcohol and water makes vanilla extract. It is more commonly used than vanilla paste or fresh vanilla pods because it is easy to find and more affordable. Just be wary when purchasing a bottle, as you really want

to avoid the imitation versions, as they tend to have a chemical and tinny aftertaste. KEEP IT NATURAL Y'ALL!

Xylitol: Xylitol is a white crystalline powder that looks like sugar. It is extracted and processed from the fibres of many fruits and vegetables. It has almost the same sweetness level as sugar but has a low Glycemic Index (GI) value, meaning it has little effect on blood sugar levels and insulin. It has become really popular with diabetics as well as those following a low-sugar diet.

Za'atar: Za'atar is a Middle Eastern spice mixture that you can basically use in or on anything. It is generally prepared using ground dried thyme, oregano, marjoram, mixed with toasted sesame seeds, salt and often times sumac. It can be used on meats, vegetables, rice and breads or as a flavouring for olive oil before dipping bread.

BREAKFAST

CHIA SEED PUDDING

Soooooo, where to begin... I think this is my favourite of all-time favourites. Be it breakfast, snack or dessert, this really is the way forward. Not only is it DEE-LISH, it is also super-filling, providing a CRAZY amount of nutrients.

MAKES 5–6 LARGE BOWLS

300g cashew nuts

750ml water

2½ tbsp honey or maple
   syrup or coconut sugar

10g coconut oil

1½ tsp vanilla extract

½ tbsp ground cinnamon

20g ground linseeds (flaxseeds)

50g chia seeds

FOR THE TOPPING

25g flaked almonds

1 mango, peeled, stoned
   and cut into cubes

4 tbsp almond butter

You will need a blender or
   food processor.

1. Soak the cashew nuts in a bowl of water for at least 4 hours, or overnight, then drain and set aside.

2. Pour the water into a large bowl and add the honey, coconut oil, vanilla, cinnamon and linseeds and stir to combine.

3. Place the soaked cashews into a blender or food processor, add the water mixture and blend until it is almost a purée. Work in batches if your blender isn't big enough. Transfer the mixture to a large bowl then whisk small batches of the linseeds and chia seeds into the mixture to prevent lumps forming. Leave to stand for 1 hour, or overnight.

4. When ready to serve, preheat the oven to 180°C/350°F/Gas mark 4.

5. For the topping, spread the almonds out on a non-stick baking sheet and roast in the hot oven for 5 minutes, or until golden. Remove and leave to cool.

6. Serve the chia seed pudding in bowls, topped with the cubed mango, toasted almonds and a spoonful of almond butter.

> Variation: If you like, you can add other natural flavourings and mix up the toppings to make delicious and different dishes.

CHESTNUT AND ALMOND WAFFLES

You really can't go wrong with waffles, especially when they're suitable for a grain-free lifestyle, are gluten-free AAAANNNDDD taste like heaven in your mouth. I have nothing more to say on the matter.

MAKES 7 BELGIAN WAFFLES

170g gluten-free chestnut
    flour or other gluten-free flour
170g almond flour or finely ground
    almonds
a pinch of salt
1¾ tsp baking powder
4 eggs
10g pure vanilla paste or
    2 vanilla pods
130g vegetable oil
50g maple syrup or honey
50ml sweetened almond
    milk
Strawberry Chia Jam (see page 36),
    fresh strawberries and
    maple syrup, to serve

You will need a waffle maker.

1. Preheat the waffle maker and spray with oil. If your waffle maker has a temperature setting, set it to 240°C/475°F.
2. Put the chestnut flour, almond flour, salt and baking powder into a large bowl and whisk to make sure there are no lumps.
3. In another bowl, stir the eggs, vanilla, oil, maple syrup and almond milk together. Add the dry ingredients and stir gently to a thick smooth batter. Don't overmix otherwise the waffles will be heavy.
4. Ladle the mixture into the waffle maker and close it. Cook until the waffle maker's indicator light shows that the cooking time is complete, or until no more steam comes out. Open the maker carefully, the waffles should be golden brown and crispy.
5. Serve the waffles with quartered fresh strawberries, strawberry jam and maple syrup.

NUTTY BIRCHER MUESLI

Ever wondered what to have for breakfast but can't actually be bothered to make anything? This is the perfect breakfast to make in advance on a Sunday night and store in your fridge to eat throughout the week. It can be stored for up to four days. Using shop-bought hazelnut milk will extend its shelf life over the homemade milk.

SERVES 4-6

75g roasted hazelnuts, crushed
200g gluten-free rolled oats
40g quinoa flakes
600ml hazelnut milk
   (shop-bought or use
   the recipe for Cacao
   Hazelnut 'Nutella' Milk
   (see page 246, just omit
   the cacao powder)
40ml honey (optional)
1 Granny Smith or tart green
   apple, finely grated
juice of 1 lemon
50g dried apricots, chopped

TO DECORATE

fresh raspberries or fresh fruit
1 tbsp Strawberry Chia Jam
   (see page 36)

1. In a bowl, stir together 50g of the roasted hazelnuts with all the other ingredients until everything is well combined. Cover and allow to soak in the fridge for a few hours or overnight. After soaking, if you find it is too thick then stir in a little more hazelnut milk until you are happy with the consistency. The mixture will thicken up after a few hours so be patient and see if you need to add more liquid.

2. In the morning, decorate with raspberries or any fresh fruits you have, the jam and the reserved crushed hazelnuts and serve.

> Note: To crush the roasted hazelnuts use a food processor or place them in a sealed plastic bag and roll a heavy rolling pin or bottle of wine over them until they are crushed.

GLUTEN-FREE GRANOLA

If you ever want to entice someone, whether it's a man or a woman, why don't you make this granola and I guarantee that heavenly smell in your kitchen will bring all the boys or girls to your yard! It's perfect to make in batches and store in an airtight container for a week or so, even if it's just to dip into for a cheeky midnight snack.

SERVES 10-12
200g pitted dates, halved
    vertically
65g goji berries
500g gluten-free rolled oats
75g buckwheat groats
100g pumpkin seeds
125g sunflower seeds
25g sesame seeds
60g coconut flakes
150g quinoa flakes
120g skin-on almonds
100g pecan nuts

FOR THE SYRUP
200ml sunflower oil
120g honey
1 tbsp vanilla paste
1 tbsp ground cinnamon

TO SERVE
Milk
Yogurt
Chopped fresh fruit

Recipe pictured overleaf.

1. Preheat the oven to 180°C/350°F/Gas mark 4.
2. Put the dates and goji berries in a small bowl and set aside.
3. Put the remaining dry ingredients in a large bowl and mix together, then set aside.
4. Put all the ingredients for the syrup into a pan and simmer over a medium–low heat for 10 minutes. Don't let the mixture boil. Remove from the heat and add the syrup mixture to the dry ingredients in the bowl (still keeping the dates and goji berries separate) and stir together until combined.
5. Spread the oat mixture out on a non-stick baking sheet in a single layer and cook in the hot oven, stirring every 10 minutes, for 30 minutes or until golden brown and crispy. Leave to cool.
6. Once cooled, add the reserved dates and goji berries to the oat mixture and combine well. Serve the granola with your choice of milk, yogurt or both, and top with some fresh fruit.

PROTEIN PANCAKES

It's in the name, bro.

MAKES 14-16 PANCAKES

2 eggs, separated

a pinch of salt

2 ripe bananas, peeled and
chopped into pieces

300g gluten-free oats

450ml almond milk

30g protein powder of your
choice, we use Sun Warrior
Raw Vegan Vanilla Protein

2 tsp vanilla extract

2 tsp bicarbonate of soda

4 tsp cream of tartar

1 tbsp coconut oil

TO FLAVOUR THE PANCAKES

100g raspberries

100g blueberries

TO SERVE (OPTIONAL)

coconut yogurt

coconut cream

fresh fruit

cacao nibs

maple syrup

You will need a blender.

1. Preheat the oven to 110°C/225°F/Gas mark ¼.
2. Whisk the egg whites with the salt in a large grease-free bowl until soft peaks form, then set aside.
3. Add the bananas and all the remaining ingredients, except the egg whites and coconut oil, to a blender and blend until smooth. Transfer to a bowl and fold in the egg whites and any fruit flavouring using a spatula.
4. Place a good non-stick pan over a medium heat. Once hot, add the coconut oil. You don't want too much oil, just enough to coat the pan. Pour the batter into the pan and tilt the pan so it covers the whole base. Once it starts to look brown, about 3–4 minutes, loosen the pancake from the base of the pan with a spatula and flip over on to the other side to cook for 2–3 minutes. Remove to an ovenproof dish, cover with foil and place in the oven to keep warm while you repeat with the remaining batter.
5. Top the pancakes with whatever you like, such as a spoonful of yogurt, some coconut cream, fresh fruit, cacao nibs and maple syrup.

> Notes: Bicarbonate of soda reacts with the acid, so if you don't have cream of tartar then add 2 tablespoons lemon juice to the almond milk and leave it to stand for a few minutes.
> If you're feeling extra lazy you can just put in the whole egg without separating the whites – the pancakes will still be good, just a bit less fluffy.

SKINNY EGGS BENEDICT

Eggs benny, but lighter, SAY WHAAAATT? The feathery yogurt saffron sauce is a perfect substitute if you're trying to keep away from the heavier, more buttery sauces like traditional hollandaise. The saffron ties in a beautiful colour and fragrance to the dish which you wouldn't normally eggspect, I can assure you it is EGG-XELLENTE! (Sorry, a couple of egg puns here were a must.)

SERVES 2

½ recipe Saffron Yogurt (see page 186)

1 small avocado

4 medium eggs (we use Clarence Court as their yolks are bright yellow!)

1 tbsp white wine vinegar

2 slices multi-seed gluten-free bread

6 cherry tomatoes, cut in half

2 sprigs of chive, finely chopped, to garnish

> Tip: Have everything ready to go before you poach your eggs – nobody likes cold eggs!

1. Start by making the Saffron Yogurt (see page 186) and set aside.

2. Cut the avocado in half, remove the stone and make .25 cm slices vertically across the flesh. Leave the flesh in the skin until you are ready to serve.

3. Make sure your eggs are fresh or they won't poach very well. You can check this by cracking it into a saucer; if the white stands up around the yolk then it is fresh, if it's watery then it is old. Fill a pan with water and 1 tablespoon white vinegar. Bring to the boil, then reduce until simmering. Lightly swirl the water with a spoon and crack an egg into the middle of the swirl or into a cup and then tip it in. Repeat the process with each egg, making sure the water is always lightly simmering. Work quickly so the eggs are all the same level of doneness. A soft poach will take 2–3 minutes and a hard poach will take 4–5. Once your eggs are poaching, toast the bread.

4. Remove the toast and place on 2 plates. Scoop out the sliced avocado. Divide the avocado and tomatoes between the toasts. Top each with 2 eggs, coat in Saffron Yogurt, garnish with chives and serve.

HEMP MILK

Got hemp milk? Don't feel mislead by the name, hemp milk is not only good for you but also extremely good for the environment! A great alternative to other non-dairy milks that are made of nuts, this still has that delicious nutty flavour.

MAKES ABOUT 3.5 LITRES

250g shelled hemp hearts
  (seeds)
2 tbsp honey or natural liquid
  sweetener of choice
1 tbsp coconut oil
3.5 litres water
1 whole vanilla pod

You will need a sterilised glass bottle or jar, a high-speed blender and a nut-milk bag or muslin cloth.

1. Add all the ingredients to a blender and blend for about 2–3 minutes, or until smooth.
2. Strain the liquid through a nut-milk bag into a wide bowl. Discard the hemp fibres remaining in the bag, then pour the milk from the bowl into a large sterilised glass bottle or jar (see page 36). Seal with a lid and store in the fridge for up to 3 days.

Note: You can use other flavourings, such as ¼ teaspoon freshly grated nutmeg or ¼ teaspoon ground cardamom instead of vanilla, if you like.

STRAWBERRY CHIA JAM

This is LITERALLY MY JAM. The addition of chia seeds not only increases your fibre intake but creates this kind of jelly-like texture which is beyond delish. She's also a keeper – three weeks in the fridge YO.

MAKES ABOUT 500G

600g strawberries, fresh or
    frozen
100g honey or coconut sugar
2 tbsp vanilla extract
1 tbsp lemon juice
finely grated zest of 1 lemon
100g chia seeds

You will need a blender and a sterilised jar.

If using fresh strawberries, hull and quarter them. Put the strawberries, honey or sugar, vanilla, lemon juice and lemon zest into a saucepan and cook over a medium heat until the mixture starts to bubble, then lower the heat and cook gently for 30 minutes.

Remove the pan from the heat and add the mixture to a blender and blitz until smooth or to your desired consistency. If you like your jam chunky then you can omit this step.

Pour the mixture back into the saucepan and stir in the chia seeds well. (You can just use the saucepan as a bowl to avoid getting another bowl dirty!)

Pour the jam into a sterilised jam jar (see note below) and leave to cool. Seal with a sterilised lid and store in the fridge for up to 3 weeks.

> **Tip:** If using frozen fruit, allow them to defrost overnight in the saucepan with the coconut sugar or honey on top.
>
> **Note:** To sterilise jars and lids, wash them in hot soapy water, rinse and then dry in an oven preheated to 130°C/250°F/Gas mark ½. Alternatively, put them in a dishwasher and make sure they are dry before using.

SO FRESH AND SO CLEAN

The cosiest, most delicious, oowey, gooey, heavenly **MOTHER** of all breakfast bowls! The poached eggs? The kale? The sweet potato? The quinoa? **THAT SPINACH CASHEW CREMAAAA?** Roasting the sweet potato is going to make your kitchen smell like a wonderland, and the thought of that gloriously runny yolk mixing in with all that goodness... **OOEEEEE.**

SERVES 4

2–3 sweet potatoes (250g), peeled and cubed

olive oil, for roasting and drizzling

sea salt

1 tbsp white wine vinegar

8 eggs

100g kale leaves, stalks removed

600g cooked quinoa (see page 161)

100g Almond Pesto (optional), (see page 185)

Spinach cashew crema (see page 188)

sesame seeds, to serve

1. Preheat the oven to 200°C/400°F/Gas mark 6.
2. Toss the sweet potatoes in 1½ tablespoons of olive oil until coated, then season with salt and lay in a single layer in a roasting tray. Roast in the hot oven for 25 minutes.
3. Meanwhile, poach your eggs (see page 34).
4. Once the sweet potato is cooked, turn off the oven and put the kale on top of the sweet potato, leaving the oven door slightly ajar. Let the residual heat of the oven wilt the kale.
5. In a large bowl, combine the sweet potato, kale, quinoa and pesto (if using) and toss together lightly with your hands or a spoon until everything is mixed together – and coated in the pesto, if using. Divide among bowls and top each with 2 poached eggs. Spoon over the spinach cashew crema and sprinkle with sesame seeds. Drizzle with olive oil and a pinch of salt.

FIG JAM

This recipe brings us back to our childhood here at The Good Life Eatery. Iranians and figs create a rather romantic combination in the kitchen, especially when it comes to making them into jam. Figs are a very special ingredient to us, as they truly embody the essence of seasonality. I remember as a kid standing in our kitchen at home watching my mum and grandma making jam for hours on end – a fantastic setting for their daily gossip sessions.

MAKES 200G

300g dried figs, diced
60ml maple syrup
20ml fresh orange juice
1½ tsp vanilla extract
½ tsp ground cinnamon

You will need a blender and a sterilised jar.

Recipe pictured on this page and overleaf.

1. To make the fig jam, place all the ingredients in a pan and cook over a low heat for 30 minutes, stirring occasionally.
2. When the mixture is thick and the figs have become soft, remove from the heat and, while still hot, put the mixture into a blender and blitz into a thick compote-like jam.
3. Set aside to cool then store in a sterilised jar (see page 36) for up to 3 weeks in the fridge.

Note: This recipe contains no added sugar, so please keep it in the fridge.

ACAI BOWL

ACAIIIII, ACAI, A-CA-I!!!! What is acai, you may ask? It's something that is pretty unfamiliar on our side of the planet. Our interest in acai was born from our Brazilian surfer friends who eat this bowl nearly every day after surfing, but it also works as a DREAM for breakfast. The acai purée is derived from a berry found in the Amazon rainforest and is EXTREMELY high in antioxidants. Fresh acai berries are pretty hard to find outside its native lands, so you will have to settle for a frozen product – but do not be alarmed, it still tastes UH-MAZING!

SERVES 4

ACAI PUREE

100g frozen acai (frozen packs found at Whole Foods or Amazon)

120g whole strawberries, hulled

75ml orange juice or any juice or almond milk

4 ripe bananas, peeled and roughly chopped

½ large avocado or 1 small, peeled, stoned and roughly chopped

15g honey (optional)

TO SERVE (per bowl)

75g Gluten-free Granola (see page 29)

¼ of the acai purée (see recipe above)

5 slices of banana

4 slices of strawberry

a sprinkle of bee pollen

4 blueberries

You will need a Vitamix or high speed blender.

1. Put the frozen acai, strawberries, juice or milk, bananas, avocado and honey, if using, into a large blender and blend until it is a smooth purée.

2. Put the granola into a serving bowl, pour the acai purée over the top, then tap the bowl gently on the work surface to make sure the purée covers the granola evenly. Arrange the fruit on top, with a sprinkle of bee pollen and serve.

LUNCH

CORN AND POLENTA FRITTERS

It's always hard to think of that 'something different' to eat for lunch, but I'm a strong believer in exploring various flavazzz from all over the world. This dish is inspired by Mexi-Cali cuisine. Having said that, I wouldn't restrict this to only lunch, it can also be a good breakfast or brunch option. Mix this up by serving the fritter without the eggs and with some mixed greens and our Dijon Vinaigrette (see page 193).

MAKES 5

½ red onion, peeled and
    roughly chopped
large pinch of chopped fresh parsley
large pinch of chopped fresh basil
200g fresh corn kernels (about
    3 corn-on-the-cobs)
200g fine polenta
2 eggs
3 tbsp olive oil
¼ tsp ground turmeric
¼ tsp smoked paprika
150ml unsweetened almond milk
salt and freshly ground
    black pepper
coconut oil, for frying

TO SERVE (per person)
½ mashed avocado
2 poached (see page 34) or
    fried eggs
dried red chilli flakes

1. Place all the ingredients, except for the coconut oil, in a large bowl and stir until combined.

2. Lightly oil a non-stick frying pan and place over a medium heat. Ladle 125g of batter into the pan, forming a round cake, and fry for 4 minutes on each side or until browned. Remove and repeat until all the mixture is used up.

3. Serve each fritter topped with the mashed avocado, a couple of eggs and a sprinkle of chilli flakes.

GRILLED SWORDFISH WITH JALAPEÑO CAPER SALSA

The only word that comes to mind here is FRESH! This is a perfect, light, summery lunch. I don't know many people who usually buy for swordfish to eat at home, so this is definitely a 'broadening your horizons' kind of recipe. The fish itself is very meaty, like a steak, and is a great source of protein. Jalapeño caper salsa is a fantastic accompaniment to this dish, and in case you haven't noticed, we are chilli freaks here at The Good Life, so EMBRACE THE BURN!

SERVES 4

4 x 150g swordfish fillets, about
   2cm thick
salt and freshly ground black pepper
olive oil, for drizzling

FOR THE JALAPEÑO SALSA

3 tbsp olive oil
½ juicy lemon
2 tbsp capers, drained
¼ tsp fennel seeds
¼ red onion (about 60g), finely
   chopped
30g pickled jalapeños, finely chopped
½ tbsp chopped dill

FOR THE LITTLE GEM SALAD

4–5 little gem hearts
juice of ½ lemon
3 tbsp olive oil

1. First, make the salsa. In a small non-stick frying pan over a high heat, add 1 tablespoon of the oil. Place the lemon half, flesh-side down, and allow it to brown until the flesh is blackened and it is softening, about 10 minutes. Remove and set aside. Add the capers and fennel seeds to the pan and fry for 4–5 minutes until the capers are crisp and the fennel seeds are toasted. Remove from the heat and set aside.

2. Put the onion and jalapeños in a bowl with the dill and remaining oil. Add the capers and fennel seeds and squeeze in the juice of the blackened lemon, then scrape out the lemon flesh. The flavour of the lemon is insane! Cover and allow to infuse while you prepare your fish.

3. Season the swordfish fillets with salt, pepper and olive oil. Heat a griddle pan or non-stick frying pan over a medium-high heat. Place the fish in the pan and sear for 3 minutes on one side. Turn over and sear for a further 3 minutes until golden.

4. Prepare a simple salad by cutting the lettuce into quarters or eighths depending on size, then put in a bowl and toss with the lemon juice, olive oil and salt and pepper to taste.

5. Serve the swordfish with a few spoonfuls of the salsa and a side of the salad.

NOTE You can prepare the salsa the day before. It is great with other white fish and grilled prawns.

SHRIMP FRIED RICE

This is definitely one of my go-to quick comfort meals (especially when I'm hungover). The secret is to use day-old cooked rice, which seems to work better. The reason for this is that the moisture content is reduced once it's been in the fridge for a day so it won't end up a mushy disaster. I obviously learnt the hard way...

SERVES 4

350g raw small prawns, peeled, deveined and butterflied
½ tbsp garlic powder
½ tsp dried red chilli
salt and freshly ground black pepper
2 tbsp coconut oil
8 spring onions, chopped
100g Tenderstem broccoli, stems and florets chopped
2 garlic cloves, peeled and chopped
1 tbsp finely chopped ginger
525g cold brown rice (see page 164)
2 large or 3 small eggs, beaten
80g peas, fresh or frozen
80g frozen podded edamame beans, thawed
1 red chilli, deseeded and finely chopped
4 tbsp tamari
2 tbsp rice vinegar
1 tsp toasted sesame oil
½ tbsp black sesame seeds, plus ½ tbsp to garnish

1. Season the prawns with the garlic powder, red chilli and salt and pepper. Heat a large frying pan over a high heat. When the pan is really hot, add 1 tablespoon of the coconut oil and allow to melt, then add the prawns and pan-fry for 3 minutes, or until they are slightly opaque in the centre. Remove the prawns from the pan and set aside.

2. Add the remaining coconut oil to the pan, reduce the heat slightly to medium–high, and add the spring onions, broccoli, garlic, ginger and the rice and stir until well combined.

3. Push the rice mixture to one side of the pan, then pour the eggs into the other side and quickly stir so they start to scramble. Start to slowly incorporate the rice mixture into the eggs, making sure that the eggs do not clump together. Add all the remaining ingredients to the pan, including the prawns. Stir well, mixing everything together for an additional 2–3 minutes, until the vegetables are cooked and the prawns are hot.

4. Garnish with some black sesame seeds and serve.

NOHO SPECIAL

I literally ate these every day for a year until Shirin removed them from the menu. The consequences of this poor decision was not only being accosted by several customers on the street, but also a deep sadness when lunchtime came around. I know what you're thinking, cauliflower and quinoa? Really? Just TRUST us, OK! They're back on the menu for a reason (happy dance). They can also be used as the perfect veggie burger recipe. Oh, and don't forget the chipotle sauce, or else!

SERVES 2–3 PEOPLE/
MAKES 6–7 PATTIES

150g cauliflower, roughly
    chopped
2 slices gluten-free bread,
    roughly torn or 25g gluten-
    free breadcrumbs
200g cooked white quinoa (see
    page 161)
40g nutritional yeast flakes
2 eggs
1 shallot (about 60g), finely
    chopped
2 garlic cloves, peeled and crushed
½ tbsp finely chopped rosemary
2 tsp sea salt
5–6 cracks of black pepper
1 tbsp olive oil, for greasing
1 quantity of Chipotle Sauce
    (see page 195), to serve

1. Preheat the oven to 200°C/400°F/Gas mark 6. Line a baking tray with greaseproof paper.

2. Blitz the roughly chopped cauliflower in a food processor until it resembles couscous. If you don't have a food processor, chop the cauliflower with a large knife or use a box grater to grate the cauliflower. Set aside in a large bowl. Blitz the bread in the food processor until crumbs form and add to the cauliflower mixture. Then add in all the remaining ingredients and mix together until well combined. The mixture will be quite wet and sticky.

3. Line a baking tray with parchment paper and lightly grease. Using your hands, make 6–7 balls. Each ball will be quite wet and won't hold its shape very well. Flatten the balls into patties and place directly onto the greased parchment paper. Bake for 30 minutes until lightly golden.

4. Serve the patties with the Chipotle Sauce and a mixed green salad dressed with our Dijon Vinaigrette (see page 193) or oil and vinegar.

> Note: These are great made in advance and can be kept in the fridge for 2 days. Simply reheat in a 200°C/400°F/Gas mark 6 oven for 5 minutes.

GREEN EGG FRITTATA

The greener the better, I say! This is good to make in batches and keep in the fridge. It's also a great all-day option, served hot or cold. The best part is that you can change the greens to fit what you fancy or keep it in tune with seasonal produce currently available at your local farmers' market. The almond pesto is bangin'!

MAKES 10 PORTIONS

8 eggs

1 medium courgette, sliced into half moons

8 asparagus spears, sliced into rounds about ½cm thick

75g kale, stalks removed and leaves chopped

4 tbsp chopped basil leaves

2 tbsp chopped fresh parsley

6 spring onions, cut into rounds about ½cm thick

2 garlic cloves, peeled and roughly chopped

½ medium fennel bulb, thinly sliced

salt and freshly ground black pepper

1 quantity of Almond Pesto (see page 185), to serve

1. You will need a 20cm round springform cake tin lined with greaseproof paper.

2. Preheat the oven to 170°C/325°F/Gas mark 3.

3. In a large bowl, crack the eggs and whisk well. Add all the remaining ingredients, stir and season really well with salt and pepper.

4. Pour the mixture into the lined cake tin and bake in the hot oven for 45–50 minutes until a knife inserted in the middle comes out clean. Remove from the oven and leave to cool.

5. When cool, remove from the tin and slice into wedges. Serve with the Almond Pesto.

> Note: You can substitute the whole eggs with 500g of egg whites.

BAKED CHICKEN DIPPAZ

CHICKAAAANNNN DIPPAZ. What's better than homemade chicken fingers? Had my mum made me homemade chicken fingers, I think I would have loved her that much more (hope you're not reading this, Mum)... Just FYI, HONEY MUSTARD = LIFE!

SERVES 4

400g chicken breasts
150g gluten-free flour
salt and freshly ground black
    pepper
pinch of red chilli powder
pinch of garlic powder
300g roasted and salted almonds,
    finely ground
3–4 eggs, lightly beaten

FOR THE OIL-FREE HONEY MUSTARD

80g natural soya yogurt
30g wholegrain mustard
30g American Yellow mustard
100g honey
1 tbsp lemon juice

1. Preheat the oven to 200°C/400°F/Gas mark 6.

2. Slice the chicken into 3–4 strips. Put the flour in a bowl large enough to hold the chicken and season generously with salt and pepper. Add the chilli and garlic powders.

3. Put the finely ground roasted and salted almonds in another bowl large enough to hold the chicken.

4. First dredge the chicken in the flour, then the egg, then the almonds and turn until coated all over.

5. Place the chicken in a roasting tin and cook in the oven for 15 minutes. You can raise the oven temperature to 220°C/425°F/Gas mark 7 for the last 5 minutes to give the chicken a nice brown colour.

6. Meanwhile, to make the honey mustard dressing, stir all the ingredients together. Set aside.

7. Serve the chicken on a large platter with the dressing in a dipping bowl.

> Note: We don't generally use soya yogurt, as we try not to use too many soya-based products, but it works really well in this dressing.

SWEET POTATO FALAFEL

Falafels have been taken to a whole new level with these little balls of happiness. They are crunchy, yet creamy, exceptional in a sandwich, with a dip or even in a salad.

MAKES ABOUT 50 SMALL FALAFEL

500g sweet potatoes, peeled
  and roughly cubed
60ml olive oil
½ tsp ground cumin
25g piece of fresh ginger,
  peeled and grated
2 garlic cloves, peeled and very
  finely chopped
½ tbsp white wine vinegar
½ tbsp harissa paste
½ red onion, peeled and finely
  chopped
salt and freshly ground black pepper
600g cooked quinoa (see page 161)

FOR THE SIMPLE YOGURT DIP
(optional)
150g natural Greek or coconut
  yogurt
4 tbsp olive oil
finely grated zest of 1 lemon
1 tbsp chopped parsley

1. Preheat the oven to 200°C/400°F/Gas mark 6 and line a baking tray with parchment paper and lightly grease it.

2. Put the sweet potatoes into a large bowl or container. Pour in the olive oil, ground cumin, ginger, garlic, vinegar, harissa paste and a little salt to season. Toss well, then arrange them on the lined baking trays in a single layer and roast in the hot oven for 12–15 minutes until the sweet potatoes are soft. Leave the oven on and line another baking tray with parchment paper, leaving it out. This tray will be for the falafels.

3. While the sweet potatoes are baking, cook the quinoa – if you haven't done so already.

4. Transfer the roasted sweet potato to a food processor and purée until smooth. If you don't have a processor, use a potato ricer, masher or the back of a fork.

5. Put the chopped onion, sweet potato mash and cooked quinoa together in a bowl and mix well. Taste and check for seasoning. Using clean, damp hands, roll the mixture into 30g balls, about the size of a golf ball. Arrange the balls on the lined baking tray and cook in the hot oven for 20 minutes until brown and crispy.

6. Meanwhile, to make the dip, mix all the ingredients together in a bowl and serve with the warm falafel.

> Tip: Enjoy these as a snack all week. Make a batch of these ahead and reheat them in a 200°C/400°F/Gas mark 6 oven for 4–5 minutes.

GLUTEN-FREE TERIYAKI SALMON

Sweet, tangy and gooey, the very best way to marinate salmon! This has been my go-to protein option in the last few years of running the eateries. I love it served on a bed of brown rice with a side of broccoli – super-filling and super-fuelling!

MAKES 250ML

4 x 240g salmon fillets

FOR THE MARINADE

2 garlic cloves, peeled and
    roughly chopped
40g piece of ginger, peeled and
    roughly chopped
30g red chilli, roughly chopped
50g banana shallots, peeled
    and roughly chopped
50ml sunflower oil
125ml tamari (gluten-free
    soy sauce)
juice of 2–3 oranges (about
    125ml)
4 tbsp honey
½ tbsp sesame oil

You will need a food processor
    or blender.

1. For the marinade, put the garlic, ginger, chilli, banana shallots and sunflower oil in a food processor or blender and blitz to a chunky paste so that there are some small bits of texture left.

2. In a bowl, combine the tamari, orange juice, honey and sesame oil.

3. Heat a frying pan over a low heat, add the paste and cook for 10 minutes until aromatic.

4. Add the tamari mixture and simmer for about 25 minutes, then remove from the heat and leave to cool. The sauce should be dark, slightly thick and sticky when cooled. Let completely cool before using.

5. Put the salmon in a shallow dish and spoon a decent amount of marinade over each piece of salmon, on the flesh side, then cover and leave to marinate for 1 hour in the refrigerator.

6. If you have any marinade leftover, you can keep it in an airtight container in the refrigerator for up to 3 weeks.

7. Preheat the oven to 220°C/425°F/Gas mark 7 and line a baking tray with parchment paper.

8. Place the salmon fillets skin-side down on the lined baking tray and cook in the hot oven for 6–8 minutes, depending on thickness, until cooked. Allow to cool slightly before serving.

> Note: This marinade is also delicious when used with beef, chicken or vegetables.

OPEN-FACED SALMON AVOCADO TOAST

One of the number 1 contenders amongst our customers at the eateries. This is definitely the perfect, filling lunch option, although I have actually noticed that boys especially love this as an afternoon snack. Super easy and if you have any leftover cooked salmon this shouldn't take longer than 5 minutes to put together. **THE LIME WEDGE CHANGES EVERYTHING!!!**

SERVES 4

4 medium avocado, stone
   removed and cut into cubes
4–6 large slices rye bread
4 cooked teriyaki salmon fillets
   (see page 64)
2 tbsp white or black sesame seeds

1. In a large bowl, lightly mash the avocado flesh with a fork so that it starts to stick together.

2. Lightly toast the rye bread and spoon avocado onto each piece of toast until it is completely covered.

3. Flake a salmon fillet over each piece of toast, spooning any leftover sauce over the top.

4. Sprinkle each piece of toast with a pinch of sesame seeds.

CRISPY SHRAMP

I am most definitely the creep that hangs out near the kitchen door at parties to wait for the appetisers to come out. I think I would end up stalking the host for more if these were being served... and that sweet chilli jam, OOOOO WEEEEEEEE!

SERVES 4

olive oil, for greasing
350g king prawns, peeled and
    deveined with tails still intact
400ml can coconut milk,
    well shaken
150g polenta
½ tbsp garlic powder
¼ tsp chilli powder
pinch of salt
200g gluten-free flour

FOR THE SWEET CHILLI SAUCE

3–4 red chillies
2 tbsp olive oil
3 garlic cloves, peeled and
    very finely chopped
1–2 shallots, finely chopped
½ tbsp rice vinegar
1 tsp salt
2 tbsp honey or natural
    liquid sweetener
200g ripe tomatoes,
    chopped
½ red pepper, deseeded
    and chopped

You will need a high-speed blender
    or food processor.

1. Preheat the oven to 220°C/425°F/Gas mark 7. First, make the chilli sauce. Rinse the chillies and blot dry. Remove and discard the stalks from the chillies, then cut in half, removing half the seeds. Using rubber gloves, finely chop the chillies. If you don't have gloves, wash your hands and knife immediately.

2. Heat the oil in a pan over a medium–high heat. Add the garlic and shallots and sauté for 1 minute, or until opaque and fragrant. Add the vinegar, salt, honey, tomatoes, pepper and chillies, then reduce the heat to low and simmer for 10–12 minutes, allowing everything to break down and the chillies to soften. Remove from the heat and allow to cool completely.

3. Once cooled, blend it in a high-speed blender or food processor until completely smooth. If it is chunky, strain through a sieve. Set aside until ready to use.

4. Lightly oil a baking tray. It is crucial to grease as the coating can stick, even if using greaseproof paper.

5. Butterfly the prawns by scoring along the outer body of the prawn, where the vein was, then pushing the flesh apart and open out like a butterfly. Make sure the prawns are very dry before coating.

6. Pour the coconut milk into a bowl. Put the polenta, garlic and chilli powders and salt into another bowl.

7. Lightly sprinkle flour over the prawns, then dip into the coconut milk, then the polenta mixture. Arrange the prawns on the tray and bake, turning halfway, for 12 minutes or until golden brown. Remove and serve immediately with the chilli sauce on the side.

> Note: Any extra sauce can be stored in an airtight container in the fridge for 1–2 weeks.

SPICY GRILLED AUBERGINES WITH SUNNY SIDE UP EGG

This is so über yummy. You would never think that aubergine and eggs would create such a masterpiece, but let me tell you, friends, they ABSOLUTELY DO! I mean the ooey gooey of the egg yolk mixed in with the honey sriracha aubergine is THA BOMB DIGGITY.

SERVES 4

1 tbsp honey
2 tbsp Sriracha sauce
½ tbsp garlic powder
3 tbsp olive oil, plus extra for cooking
600g aubergine (2–3 medium)
4–8 eggs (depending on how hungry
   you are!)
1–2 avocados
2 tbsp chopped coriander leaves
1 tbsp pickled jalapeños, chopped

1. Preheat the oven to 130°C/250°F/Gas mark ½.

2. In a large bowl, combine the honey, Sriracha sauce, garlic powder and olive oil.

3. Slice the aubergine into 1cm thick slices. Add the aubergine slices to the bowl of marinade and toss until generously coated.

4. Heat a non-stick pan over a medium–high heat. Add a dash of olive oil, then add the sliced aubergines. Cook them on one side until they are nicely brown and caramelised. Flip over and cook the other side. Transfer the nicely caramelised aubergines to an ovenproof plate and keep warm in the oven while you cook the eggs.

5. Just wipe the pan, add a dash of olive oil, then crack in the eggs and cook them to your preference. I like them nice and runny for this dish.

6. Remove the aubergine from the oven and lay them flat on a serving plate. Peel, stone and slice the avocados and arrange them on top of the aubergine. Top with the fried eggs, coriander leaves and pickled jalapeños and serve.

> Note: You can purchase Sriracha sauce online and will find pickled jalapeños in the Mexican section of your supermarket.

THAI LETTUCE CHICKEN CUPS

Little morsels of carb-free health and happiness come to mind when I hear the words lettuce cups. We decided to go with an Asian flavour to prove to all you wonderful home cooks that stepping out of your comfort zone can create something awesome.

SERVES 4

75g courgette, roughly chopped
50g white button mushrooms
2 kaffir lime leaves
½ red chilli, deseeded
5g fresh ginger
10g fresh coriander
2 garlic cloves, peeled
2 tbsp red Thai curry paste
2 tbsp lime juice
2 tbsp honey
1½ tbsp tamari or soy sauce
2½ tbsp sesame oil
100ml water
2 tbsp coconut oil
375g white chicken mince
3–4 heads of Baby Gem lettuce,
    leaves removed
fresh sliced red chilli, to garnish

FOR THE DIPPING SAUCE

100g mirin or rice vinegar
250ml tamari or soy sauce
100ml sesame oil
150g honey
25g piece of ginger, peeled
40g garlic cloves, peeled

TO SERVE

Avocado butter (see page 189)

You will need a food processor.

Recipe pictured overleaf.

1. To make the dipping sauce, put all the ingredients into a saucepan and bring to the boil. Allow the sauce to boil rapidly for 5 minutes, then transfer to a blender and blend until smooth. Now you want to remove all the bits, so pass the sauce through a fine sieve. Leave to cool and it's ready to serve with the lettuce cups.

2. Put the courgette, mushrooms, lime leaves, chilli, ginger, coriander and garlic into a food processor and pulse a few times until everything is in small pieces. You do not want to make a paste. Set aside.

3. Stir the curry paste, lime juice, honey, tamari, sesame oil and water in another bowl. Set aside.

4. Place a large saucepan over a high heat. Melt 1 tablespoon of coconut oil, then add the chicken mince and cook until slightly browned, about 3–4 minutes. Lower the heat to medium–high. Add all the pulsed vegetables and cook for a further 3–4 minutes then add all the wet ingredients. Cook for about 15 minutes, or until the liquid has almost fully absorbed then remove the pan from the heat and leave to cool.

5. To serve, place the lettuce cups on a serving plate and smear a spoonful of avocado butter along the leaf. Add a spoonful of the chicken mince and top with a few pieces of red chilli and some dipping sauce. Fold like a taco and enjoy!

THE GOOD LIFE SALAD

WARNING: If you don't like kale **DO NOT** attempt to make this recipe.

Shout out to our most popular salad, the combination of textures and flavours come together very nicely in making this the BEST KALE SALAD EVAAAAA. Oh, and don't be frightened by the nutritional yeast flakes, the first time I saw them, I thought it was fish food too... but they actually give a delightful cheesy tang to finish the dish off. Unexpected, I know.

SERVES 4

200g Puy lentils

2–3 sweet potatoes (750g), peeled and cubed

1 tbsp olive oil, plus extra for roasting

sea salt and freshly ground black pepper

5–6 handfuls of kale (300g), stalks removed and leaves chopped into small pieces

½ pomegranate, kernels removed

150g cooked red or black quinoa (optional)

60g walnuts, chopped

2 tbsp nutritional yeast flakes

FOR THE ORANGE AND TAHINI DRESSING

finely grated zest of 1 large orange

juice of 2 oranges

100g tahini

75ml olive oil

salt and freshly ground black pepper

1. Preheat the oven to 180°C/350°F/Gas mark 4.

2. Put the lentils in a saucepan and add 600ml water to cover the lentils completely. Bring to the boil then reduce the heat and simmer for 25 minutes, or until tender. Drain in a colander and run under cold water to stop the cooking process, then leave to cool. Set aside.

3. Put the sweet potatoes into a large bowl, add the olive oil, salt and pepper and toss well until the sweet potatoes are coated. Transfer the sweet potatoes to a roasting tin and roast in the hot oven for 15–20 minutes. Leave to cool.

4. To make the dressing, put all the ingredients into a blender and blitz until smooth or whisk by hand. Set aside.

5. Put the chopped kale leaves into a large bowl, add 1 tablespoon olive oil, and using your hands, massage the oil into the kale.

6. Once the sweet potato and lentils have cooled, add them to the kale then add the pomegranate kernels. If using quinoa, add this now. Pour in 150ml of the dressing, or to your liking, and toss until everything is coated in the dressing. Top with the chopped walnuts and nutritional yeast flakes and serve.

Variation: Add some salmon teriyaki (see page 64) or grilled chicken for extra protein.

CAESAR NON-CAESAR

I've always been rather sceptical of tampering with the classical greats – in this case the almighty Caesar salad! I'm going out on a limb here and against all my foodie morals and saying that IT BLOODY WORKS! Give it a go.

SERVES 4–5

3 skinless chicken breasts
sea salt and freshly ground
    black pepper
nutritional yeast flakes, for
    sprinkling

FOR THE VEGAN CAESAR DRESSING

200g cashew nuts
1 tbsp nutritional yeast flakes
1 tbsp low-sodium soy sauce
1 tbsp apple cider vinegar
60g white miso paste
a piece of nori sheet, the size
    of the palm of your hand
4 tbsp water
a few cracks of black pepper

FOR THE SALAD

1 garlic clove, peeled
3 slices of gluten-free bread
2 tbsp olive oil
4 handfuls of curly kale,
    chopped
3 heads of baby gem lettuce,
    chopped into 2cm pieces
10 cherry tomatoes, halved
10 olives

You will need a blender.

1. Preheat the oven to 200°C/400°F/Gas mark 6.

2. For the dressing, soak the cashews in a bowl of boiling water for 1 hour, then drain. Put the soaked cashews and remaining dressing ingredients in a blender and blitz until smooth. Set aside.

3. Cut the garlic in half and rub it on each slice of bread. Cut the bread into squares, put in a bowl, add 1 tablespoon olive oil and toss until the bread is coated in the oil. Season with salt and pepper and place on an oven tray. Bake for 15 minutes, tossing every 5 minutes.

4. Put the kale in a bowl, add the remaining olive oil and a pinch of salt, and using clean hands, massage the oil into the kale until it is coated. Set aside.

5. Season the chicken with salt and pepper. Heat 1 tablespoon of coconut oil in a griddle or frying pan over a medium-high heat. Add the chicken and fry on each side for 3–4 minutes until nicely golden, then reduce heat to medium low and allow to continue to cook through for another 3–4 minutes. Remove the chicken from the pan, leave to cool slightly, then cut the chicken into thin slices.

6. Put all the salad ingredients in a large bowl, including the croutons and kale, add the dressing (you will have some left over) and toss together until everything is coated. Add the sliced chicken and sprinkle with some nutritional yeast flakes. Serve with extra dressing, if you like.

LENTIL AND QUINOA SALAD

Warming for the soul and super filling for the belly, this salad creates an air of autumn. I never usually jump at the opportunity of using lentils as the basis of my salad, due to the fact that lentils are rather boring, and let's be honest, not so pretty. But **FEAR NOT GOOD PEOPLE**, in this scenario the sharp differences between the vinaigrette, the sweetness of the apples and the lentils really do make the dish beautifully vibrant.

SERVES 6-8

2 heads of Little Gem lettuce, only the light crunchy leaves
300g Puy lentils
2 apples, ideally Pink Ladies
juice of ½ lemon
450g cooked red quinoa or any other colour (see page 161)
2 celery sticks, halved vertically and chopped into ½cm pieces
4 spring onions, chopped into ½cm pieces
15 cherry tomatoes, halved
3 tbsp chopped fresh tarragon
3 tbsp chopped fresh parsley

FOR THE SHERRY VINAIGRETTE

3 tbsp sherry vinegar
1½ tbsp honey mustard
125ml olive oil
salt and freshly ground black pepper

TO GARNISH

80g roasted almonds
40ml balsamic glaze (optional)

1. For the sherry vinaigrette, combine the sherry vinegar and honey mustard together in a bowl. Whisk well and while whisking, slowly add the oil until it is all incorporated. Season to taste with salt and pepper and set aside.

2. Cook the Puy lentils (see page 76).

3. Remove the core from the apples and cut into small cubes. Put it into a bowl and add the lemon juice. Toss to coat. This is to prevent the apples turning brown.

4. Put all the remaining salad ingredients, including the apple and Puy lentils, in a large bowl, add the dressing and toss together until everything is coated and well combined. Top with the roasted almonds and a drizzle of the balsamic glaze, if using, and serve.

PULLED CHICKEN AND CUCUMBER SALAD

The level of freshness achieved with this salad is beyond describable – the pickled cucumber, crunchy raw cabbage and curried chicken combo is just OOOOOF. The dressing is the real kicker for me as it brings a creamy richness to create a complete well-rounded meal. Be certain of the fact that you'll be full after a bowl of this goodness.

SERVES 2-3

¼ white cabbage, finely
   chopped
100g celery sticks with leaves,
   cut into 3–4mm thick pieces
2 spring onions, cut into
   2–3mm thick slices
small handful of mint leaves,
   finely chopped, to garnish

FOR THE CURRIED CHICKEN

2 boneless skinless chicken
   breasts
1½ tbsp melted coconut oil
½ tsp curry powder
½ tsp ground turmeric
salt and freshly ground black
   pepper

FOR THE PICKLED CUCUMBER

200g English cucumber
2 tbsp rice vinegar
½ tsp sea salt
1 tsp honey
1 tsp black sesame seeds

FOR THE COCONUT CURRY DRESSING

80ml coconut cream
½ tsp curry powder
¼ tsp ground turmeric
1 tbsp lime juice (about 1 lime)
1 tbsp almond butter
1 tbsp water
salt and freshly ground black
   pepper

A mandoline is recommended.

Recipe continued overleaf.

PULLED CHICKEN AND CUCUMBER SALAD CONTINUED

1. Start by seasoning the chicken breasts with ½ tablespoon of coconut oil, curry powder, turmeric and salt and pepper. Massage in well with your hands and let the flavours infuse for 2–3 minutes.

2. Melt the remaining coconut oil in a frying pan over a medium heat and lightly brown the chicken for 4–5 minutes on each side or until fully cooked through. Remove from the pan and place on a plate or board. Using 2 forks, immediately pull the flesh apart, shredding the warm chicken, then set aside and cover.

3. For the pickled cucumber, using a mandoline or sharp knife, slice the cucumber into 1mm slices. Put the slices into a small bowl, then add the rice vinegar, sea salt and honey and toss well. Cover and leave to marinate for 10–15 minutes.

4. Meanwhile, make the dressing. Combine all the ingredients in a bowl, stir well and season to taste, then set aside.

5. To assemble the salad, drain the excess juice from the cucumber, then add the sesame seeds and toss until the cucumber is coated. Pile the cabbage into one section of a large serving bowl, pile the celery next to it in another section, then put the chicken in the next section and, lastly add the cucumber, leaving a space in the centre. Pile the spring onion in the middle, garnish with mint and drizzle the dressing over the top. Enjoy.

POACHED TUNA AND LAMB'S LETTUCE SALAD

Poaching isn't your usual technique when it comes to cooking tuna steak but we think it brings a totally different level of curiosity to your everyday tuna salad. I am kind of over the whole grilled and seared tuna scene these days, I find it to be an old-school way of opting for a healthy lunch, so let's try something new... and lamb's lettuce has to be my favourite green OF ALL TIME.

SERVES 4-6

60ml olive oil, plus extra
   for drizzling
about 500ml water or
   more to cover
juice of 1 lemon (keep the
   juiced lemon halves)
10–15 thyme sprigs
1 tbsp sea salt
½ tbsp black peppercorns
3 tuna steaks (about 120g each)
a few slices of gluten-free
   bread, toasted, to serve
1 quantity of House Shallot
   Dressing (see page 192),
   to serve

FOR THE SALAD

200g French beans, trimmed
35g sunflower seeds
50g lamb's lettuce
1 head of lettuce (about 150g)
2 medium avocados, peeled,
   stoned and diced
10 small radishes, sliced into
   rounds
10 cherry tomatoes, cut in half
1 small handful of curly
   parsley, chopped

Recipe continued and pictured overleaf.

POACHED TUNA AND LAMB'S LETTUCE SALAD CONTINUED

1. Place the olive oil, water, lemon juice, thyme, sea salt and peppercorns in a wide saucepan, that has at least a 2-litre capacity. Lay the tuna steaks flat so that they are completely covered in the liquid. Bring to a boil then reduce the heat to a simmer and cook for 6–8 minutes. You want the tuna slightly pink in the centre.

2. Remove the tuna and place it on a plate. Lightly drizzle the tuna with olive oil until it is all completely coated. This will prevent the tuna from drying out.

3. For the salad, rinse out the saucepan and fill it three-quarters full with water. Add a generous seasoning of salt and bring to the boil. Add the French beans and cook for 5 minutes, or until the beans are tender but still crunchy. Immediately drain and rinse under cold water to stop the cooking process then set aside.

4. Toast the sunflower seeds in a dry pan over a medium–low heat for a few minutes, stirring frequently, until they smell fragrant and toasty. Remove from the heat and set aside.

5. Put the lettuces, avocados, radishes, cherry tomatoes, French beans, chopped parsley and toasted sunflower seeds into a large salad bowl. Using your fingers or a fork, flake the tuna over the lettuce. Drizzle the dressing over and serve with a few slices of toasted gluten-free bread.

Note: You can store the tuna for up to 2 days in the fridge, just make sure it is generously coated in olive oil.

WARM SPINACH SALAD

EGGS ON A SALAD!!! You might be thinking that this is not a salad, but listen here, what's wrong with adding a little extra protein to make it that much more satisfying? It is also derived from a classic French recipe, believe it or not – gloriously light, yet still getting all those well-balanced nutrients.

SERVES 4

4 eggs

1 tbsp olive oil

100g purple onion, finely
    sliced into strips

60g flaked almonds

200g baby spinach, washed
    and dried

200g cherry tomatoes, halved

200g white button mushroom,
    finely sliced

FOR THE WARM BALSAMIC
DRESSING

60ml balsamic vinegar

120ml olive oil

1½ tbsp Dijon mustard

salt and freshly ground
    black pepper

1. Start by putting the eggs in a pan and pouring in enough water to cover. Bring the water to the boil, then reduce the heat and simmer for 8 minutes. When they are soft–boiled, drain, run under cool water for a few minutes and then peel and cut into quarters. Set aside.

2. Heat the oil in a medium non-stick frying pan over a medium–high heat. Add the purple onion and lightly fry for 5–7 minutes until softened and lightly golden. Set aside.

3. Wipe the frying pan with kitchen paper, set back over a medium–low heat and add the flaked almonds. Toast for 4–5 minutes until golden, then set aside.

4. Put the baby spinach, cherry tomatoes, mushrooms and sautéed purple onion into a large salad bowl. Top with the quartered eggs and toasted almonds.

5. Put all the dressing ingredients in a small saucepan and whisk vigorously over a medium–low heat for 3–4 minutes until it thickens. It should be lightly simmering as you are whisking. When ready to eat, pour the warm dressing over and serve.

Variation: To make this dish into a substantial meal, poach 8 eggs (see page 34). Serve the salad in individual portions with 2 eggs on top of each and the warm dressing drizzled over.

FARRO AND FENNEL SALAD

Fennel is just the best thing for digestion. EVER. I think this is the Iranian in me talking again (or maybe I'm just getting old) but a fennel a day really does keep your digestion on point. I never used to be a fan of fennel, I think it's due to my deep hatred towards anything aniseed, but for some reason the flavour combo here rubs me the right way. We love the balance of ingredients from the farro, cucumber and salmon and are truly EXCITED for you to try it!

SERVES 3–4

olive oil, for cooking
2 garlic cloves, peeled and crushed
200g farro or pearled spelt
1 litre water
salt and freshly ground black
    pepper
150g Persian cucumber or
    English cucumber (the
    thinner the better!)
1 large fennel bulb (about
    200g)
4 x 120g skin on salmon fillets
salt and freshly ground black
    pepper
olive oil, for coating
2 tbsp dill fronds, plus extra
    to garnish

FOR THE LEMON VINAIGRETTE

1 tbsp grainy mustard
1 tsp honey
juice of 1 lemon
75ml olive oil
salt and freshly ground black pepper

You will need a mandoline.

1. In a casserole dish over a medium heat, add a dash of olive oil, the garlic and farro and cook for 3–4 minutes until the farro and garlic are lightly toasted and browned. Don't let them burn. Pour in the water and a pinch of salt and bring to the boil. Cook for 10–15 minutes, or according to the instructions on the farro packet, then drain and set aside.

2. Using a mandoline or knife, slice the cucumber into 1cm rounds. If you are using an English cucumber, cut the rounds into half moons.

3. Meanwhile, prepare the fennel. Have a bowl of iced water nearby. Depending on size, cut the fennel in half or quarters vertically. Don't cut on the horizontal as it will ruin the beautiful shape. Using a mandoline or knife, thinly slice vertically and drop it into the iced water.

4. Heat a frying pan to medium–high. Season the salmon and lightly oil the skin. Pan-fry skin-side down for 5–6 minutes until crispy. Flip over and grill for 1 minute until cooked.

5. Meanwhile, prepare the vinaigrette. Combine the mustard, honey and lemon juice in a bowl and then slowly whisk in the olive oil until it is well combined. Season with salt and pepper.

6. Drain the fennel. Arrange the fennel, cucumber, farro, dill and vinaigrette on a serving plate. Remove and discard the skin of the salmon and lightly break the salmon over the top. Garnish with extra dill.

HARVEST SALAD

Autumn in all its glory! The peppery tones of the rocket mixed in with the deep earthy flavours of the roasted butternut squash creates the most beautifully vibrant autumn salad. It is exceptionally delicious when served with roast beef, lamp chops OR JUST ON ITS OWN.

SERVES 4

400g pearled spelt or
   Italian farro
1 low-sodium vegetable
   stock cube
salt and freshly ground
   black pepper
½ butternut squash
   (about 500g)
2 tbsp olive oil
1 tbsp honey
5 thyme sprigs or ½ tbsp
   dried thyme
80g rocket leaves
2 quantities of Caramelised
   Onions (see page 174)
1 quantity of Lemon Sage
   Vinaigrette (see page 193)

TO GARNISH

100g pomegranate seeds (about
   ½ pomegranate)
80–100g feta cheese, crumbled

1. Preheat the oven to 200°C/400°F/Gas mark 6.

2. Start by cooking the spelt according to the packet instructions. Use the vegetable stock and 2 pinches of salt to season the cooking water, then drain and set aside until ready to use.

3. Cut the butternut squash in half vertically so that you have 2 symmetrical halves. Scrape out the seeds with a spoon and discard, then lay the squash on a chopping board flesh-side down. Cut into 1cm-thick half moons and put into a large bowl. Add the olive oil, honey, thyme and sea salt and toss to coat then arrange in a single layer on a large baking tray. Roast in the hot oven for 20 minutes and leave to cool slightly.

4. To assemble your salad, start by arranging half of the butternut squash on a small serving platter, then half of the rocket, half of the spelt and half of the Balsamic Onions, then repeat with the remaining ingredients. Drizzle the dressing over the dish and garnish with pomegranate seeds and crumbled feta.

GRILLED VEGETABLE SALAD

Mmmm, I love me some grilled veggies! Grilling vegetables can bring an entirely new level of excitement to a salad; at least it does for me. Don't you find that you always end up making the same three salads at home, over and over and over again? Well, this is the perfect way to mix things up a little. You can see how well this works with the contrast of texture between the raw baby gem lettuce and the grilled vegetables.

SERVES 4

2 large courgettes, cut into
  sticks
1 bunch of spring onions,
  cut into 4cm pieces
150g Tenderstem broccoli,
  trimmed and cut into
  4cm pieces
salt and freshly ground
  black pepper
2 tbsp olive oil, for sprinkling
2 corn-on-the cobs, kernels
  removed
1 fennel bulb, halved and cut
  into very thin slices
15 cherry tomatoes, halved
4 heads of baby gem lettuce,
  finely chopped
½ head of radicchio, quartered
  and finely chopped
50g rocket
4–5 pieces of palm hearts
handful of fresh tarragon, chopped
handful of fresh parsley, chopped
1 quantity of Dijon Vinaigrette
  (see page 193), optional

1. Preheat the oven to 180°C/350°F/Gas mark 4.

2. Put the courgette, spring onions and broccoli into a roasting tray, season well with sea salt and cracked black pepper and toss in olive oil. Roast in the oven for 20 minutes.

3. Meanwhile, in a large bowl, add the corn kernels, fennel, cherry tomatoes, lettuce, radicchio, rocket, palm hearts and herbs.

4. Remove the vegetables from the roasting tray and leave to cool. Once cool, combine with the raw vegetables in the bowl and add a drizzle of the vinaigrette, if using, then serve.

> **Tip:** If you have a mandoline, use it to cut the fennel into very thin slices.
>
> **Variation:** Mix it up – use seasonal produce to keep it fresh and locally sourced all year round.

STEAK SALAD

I really can't decide which part of this EPIC recipe to start with. YOU BETTER GET YOUR MARINADE ONNNN, but do try to prep the day before, as it'll taste just that much better. Mouthwatering steak on a bed of lettuce with the most explosive flavours pulsing through your taste buds. PREACH.

SERVES 6

3 sirloin steaks (about 250g each)
salt and freshly ground black pepper
2 tbsp olive oil, plus a drizzle extra
200g shallots, thinly sliced

FOR THE STEAK MARINADE

¼ tbsp dried oregano
½ tbsp garlic powder
1 tbsp soy sauce
2 tbsp Worcestershire sauce
2 tbsp olive oil
juice of 1 lime (about 1½ tbsp)

FOR THE CARAWAY DRESSING

2 tbsp Worcestershire sauce
juice of 1 lime (about 1½ tbsp)
½ tbsp Dijon mustard
1 tsp caraway seeds
½ tbsp honey
60ml olive oil

FOR THE SALAD

1 large round lettuce, torn
80g radishes, finely sliced
125g cucumber, finely chopped
2 medium avocados, peeled, stoned and cut into cubes
2 tbsp tarragon leaves

1. Start by marinating the steaks. Put the steaks and all of the marinade ingredients into a sealable food bag, season with salt and pepper, seal, shake and chill for at least 1 hour. Allow the steaks to come to room temperature before cooking.

2. Meanwhile, make the dressing by putting the Worcestershire sauce, lime juice, Dijon mustard, caraway seeds, honey and some salt and pepper in a bowl. Whisk together then, while continuing to whisk, slowly drizzle in the olive oil until it is emulsified. Set aside.

3. Heat 2 tablespoons of olive oil in a frying pan over a medium–high heat. Add the shallots and fry on medium heat for 4–5 minutes until golden brown, then remove the shallots and set aside until ready to serve. Wipe the pan clean in order to use it for the steaks.

4. Reheat the pan over a high heat. When it is really hot, remove the steaks from the plastic bag, add a drizzle of olive oil to the pan and add the steaks. Cook in batches if there is not enough room in the pan. Grill the steaks for 6–7 minutes for medium, about 3–4 minutes on each side.

5. Assemble all the salad ingredients in a large bowl and put the shallots on top. Drizzle the dressing over and add the sliced steak. Enjoy.

> Note: Marinate your steak a day in advance or in the morning, it's even better!

WARM BUDDHA BOWL

On the precipice of being Iranian, we are rice and meat **FIEENNNDZZZ**. Rice, meat and some vegetables have been a staple go-to option for pretty much every meal (excluding breakfast) our entire lives. We truly believe a meal is incomplete without such a balance and I myself never feel full if one of the components are not involved – **LITERALLY** this is a warm, cosy, little bowl of happiness!

SERVES 4–6/
MAKES ABOUT 24 MEATBALLS

FOR THE MEATBALLS
500g minced beef fillet
25g mint leaves, finely chopped
40g parsley, leaves and stems
    finely chopped
½ red onion (about 50g), peeled
    and finely chopped
1 egg
finely grated zest of 1 lemon
2 garlic cloves, peeled and
    crushed or finely chopped
salt and freshly ground black
    pepper
2 tbsp olive oil, for frying
1 quantity Tomato Sauce (see
    page 134)
4–6 tbsp Greek yogurt, to serve
Pea Slaw (see page 161), to serve

FOR THE BROWN RICE
300g brown rice
a generous pinch of salt

1. For the meatballs, put all the ingredients, except the oil, into a large bowl and mix together well until combined. Using clean, damp hands, roll the mixture into 30g balls, about the size of a golf ball.

2. Make or heat the Tomato Sauce in a large saucepan over a low–medium heat.

3. Heat a large frying pan with a splash of olive oil over a medium heat. When hot, add the meatballs and cook for 10–12 minutes until they are lightly browned all over. Put the cooked meatballs into the tomato sauce and leave to simmer gently for 20–30 minutes while you prepare the rice.

4. To cook the rice, put the brown rice into a large saucepan, add enough water and a generous pinch of salt and bring to the boil. Cover with a lid, reduce the heat and simmer for about 30 minutes, or until rice is tender. This is a super-simple brown rice and doesn't need much flavour as everything else has lots of flavour.

5. To serve, put a large spoonful of brown rice into a bowl. Top with 4–6 meatballs per person, some tomato sauce and a tablespoon of Greek yogurt. Serve each with a small portion of the Pea Slaw. Garnish with the remaining parsley.

CORN AND QUINOA RISOTTO

This risotto has a smooth, velvety texture and is the perfect option for a light, meat-free dinner. This dish resulted from a late-night arrival from the airport. Literally, the only things I had in the cupboard were quinoa, sweetcorn and almond milk. I thought I might as well give it a go, ET VOILA!

SERVES 3

225g corn kernels (or if using
   tinned, make sure it's organic,
   salt- and sugar-free)
300ml unsweetened almond
   milk
a pinch of chilli powder
1 tbsp olive oil
1 garlic clove, peeled and crushed
½ yellow onion, peeled and
   finely chopped
1 tbsp white wine
120g uncooked quinoa, preferably
   mixed colours of red, black
   and white
salt and freshly ground black pepper
1 tbsp chopped chives, to garnish

You will need a blender.

1. To make the corn milk, blend 150g of the corn with the almond milk and chilli powder in a blender until smooth. Set aside in a jug.

2. Heat the olive oil in a saucepan over a low heat and allow it to melt. Add the garlic to the pan with the chopped onion and fry for 4–5 minutes until lightly golden. Add the white wine and stir with a wooden spoon to remove any crispy bits from the base of the pan, then add the quinoa and stir to combine.

3. Add the remaining 75g corn to the pan then pour in the corn milk. Bring to the boil then reduce the heat and simmer for about 20 minutes, stirring every few minutes until the quinoa is tender and you can see the 'tails'. Season with salt and pepper, garnish with chives and serve.

Protein hit! Serve with a pan-fried cod fillet (see page 132).

TOMATO AND COCONUT SOUP

This isn't a standard tomato soup and you will definitely achieve that velvety MmmMmMmMMMmmm with the coconut milk. It is the optimal quick and easy soup to make as I'm sure most of y'all avid home 'cookerinos' will have all these ingredients in your cupboards and fridge already – **COMFORT FOOD** to another level.

SERVES 4-5

2 tbsp coconut oil

2 yellow onions (about 300g), cut into quarters

4 large garlic cloves, peeled and smashed to release the flavour

40g piece fresh ginger, roughly chopped

2 red chillies, deseeded and roughly chopped

1 tsp ground turmeric

900g tomatoes, cut into quarters (any variety will do)

2 x 400ml tin coconut milk

200ml water

sea salt

1 tsp chopped coriander leaves, to garnish

You will need a blender.

1. Heat the oil in a medium casserole dish over a medium heat. Once it has melted, add the onions, garlic, ginger, chillies and turmeric and sweat for 5–6 minutes until the onions are soft.

2. Add the tomatoes, coconut milk and water and continue to cook for 20 minutes until the tomatoes soften and release their juices.

3. Carefully pour the mixture (it will be hot) into a blender and blend until completely smooth. Season to taste with sea salt and serve garnished with chopped coriander.

CHILLI 'NON' CARNE

Chilli no meat, she says. Most chilli eaters would consider this a sacrilege but I don't agree. This is the most incredible recipe for non-vegetarians and vegetarians alike, and that depth of flavour will be making you come back for seconds (and in my case, thirds.)

SERVES 6

200g walnuts
200g carrots, roughly chopped
1 red onion (about 200g),
    roughly chopped
150g courgette, roughly
    chopped
25g finely chopped parsley
25g finely chopped coriander
2 tbsp olive oil
4 garlic cloves, peeled and crushed
¼ tsp ground cinnamon
¼ tsp smoked paprika
½ tsp ground cumin
1 x 400g tin kidney beans,
    drained and rinsed
1 x 400g tin chickpeas, drained
    and rinsed
1 corn on the cob, kernels removed
2 x 400g tin chopped tomatoes

TO GARNISH

coconut yogurt
1 avocado, peeled, stoned and
    cut into slices
1 lime, cut into wedges
a few coriander leaves

You will need a food processor.

1. Start by rinsing the walnuts in warm water to remove any grit.

2. Drain and pulse in a food processor until finely ground, or finely chop with a knife until it resembles mince. Remove and set aside. In the same food processor, add the carrots, onion, courgette and herbs and pulse until finely chopped.

3. In a large stockpot, add the olive oil, garlic, ground walnuts, cinnamon, paprika and cumin and stir together. Add the onions, courgette, carrots and chopped herbs and cook over a low heat for 10 minutes. The onions should start to soften and there will be an amazing aroma. Stir occasionally to ensure the spices do not burn.

4. Add the kidney beans, chickpeas and corn kernels to the pot together with the tinned tomatoes and allow everything to come to a simmer, then cover and reduce the heat to very low. Cook gently for 45 minutes, stirring every 10–15 minutes to make sure it doesn't stick to the base of the pot. The chilli is ready when the tomato juice has evaporated and the flavours have developed.

5. Serve immediately, each bowl topped with a dollop of coconut yogurt, 3 slices of avocado, a lime wedge and a few coriander leaves.

BUTTERNUT SQUASH AND AUBERGINE STEW

DRIED SOUR LEMON PARTAYYYYYY. OK, I'm nearly 100 per cent sure that some of you will not have encountered this ingredient before and I know it won't be the easiest to acquire, but just get your adventure boots on because I cannot even begin to express the flavour rollercoaster you are about to embark on. If you can't find dried sour lemons this recipe is still super-flavoursome, so don't be alarmed.

SERVES 3-4

2 tbsp olive oil

1 large aubergine (about 250g),
    cut into 2–3cm cubes

150g yellow onions, cut in half
    and then into long thin strips

3 garlic cloves, peeled and crushed

200g butternut squash, peeled
    and into 2–3cm cubes

½ tsp cumin seeds

¼ tsp ground turmeric

2 tbsp tomato purée

2–3 dried sour lemons, pierced
    2–3 times (optional)

200g cherry tomatoes, cut
    in half

60g kale, roughly chopped

1 tsp roughly chopped mint

1 tsp roughly chopped coriander
    leaves

1 tsp roughly chopped tarragon

25g barberries

natural yogurt or coconut yogurt,
    to serve

1. Heat a large heavy-based pot or casserole dish over a medium–high heat. Once hot, add the olive oil, aubergine, onions and garlic, butternut squash, cumin seeds, turmeric and sauté for 10 minutes until the vegetables are nicely golden but not burning.

2. Add the tomato purée and dried sour lemons (if using) and stir until well combined and fragrant. Pour in enough water to just cover and cook for 20 minutes over a medium heat until the water starts to evaporate.

3. Add the cherry tomatoes, kale, herbs and barberries and continue to cook for another 10 minutes.

4. Top with a dollop of yogurt.

5. Serve with Brown Rice (see page 164) or Quinoa (see page 161) or with a piece of warm flatbread.

> Tip: If you can't find dried sour lemons, add a squeeze of lemon juice before serving.
>
> Tip: Again, if you can't find barberries, substitute them with dried cranberries.

CANNELLINI BEAN AND CORN SOUP

Creamy, but WITH NO CREAAAAAM. I've always found it difficult to find good soup recipes without the added heaviness of creams and butter, but in this case you can still achieve such a texture without having to surrender. You might think almond milk... weird... but so yummy you're gonna want to eat the bowl too! This is great eaten straight away but even better when left until the next day.

SERVES 4–6

1 tbsp olive oil or coconut oil
4 garlic cloves, peeled and crushed
150g white onion, finely
    chopped
4–5 celery sticks (about 100g),
    chopped
1 bay leaf
60ml white wine (optional)
200g potatoes, peeled and cut
    into 2.5cm cubes
500ml vegetable stock
200ml unsweetened almond
    milk
1 x 400g tin cannellini beans
2 corn-on-the-cobs, kernels
    removed (about 150g)
salt and freshly ground black
    pepper
flat or curly parsley leaves,
    chopped, to garnish
slice of homemade bread or
    Everything Crackers (see
    page 201), to serve

1. In a large casserole dish over a medium–low heat, add the oil with the garlic, onion, celery and bay leaf and allow to sweat for 10 minutes until the onion is translucent. Don't let it burn.

2. Add the white wine (if using), half of the cannellini beans, the potato cubes, vegetable stock and almond milk. Increase the heat to medium–high and bring just to the boil. Reduce the heat and simmer for 20 minutes, or until the potatoes are soft enough to crush with the back of a fork. Lightly crush the potatoes and beans, leaving some still slightly chunky.

3. Add the remaining white beans and corn to the pot and simmer for another 20 minutes, stirring every few minutes. Season with salt and pepper and garnish with the parsley. Serve with homemade bread or Everything Crackers.

MISO PRAWN NOODLE SOUP

Comfort in a bowl, you say? YES PLEASE! A pot full of this, piping hot, when I'm not feeling well is the only thing I crave. See, miso soup doesn't have to be boring... it's good for the soul!

SERVES 4-5

1 litre water

110g white miso paste

150g buckwheat noodles

20 small raw prawns, butterflied

150g beansprouts

200g smoked tofu, cut into 2cm cubes

20g nori seaweed, cut into thin 4cm strips

2 tbsp coriander leaves

1 red chilli, thinly sliced

2 tbsp sesame seeds

1 lime, cut into wedges

FOR THE ROASTED CABBAGE

½ head Savoy cabbage (about 700g), cut into 5mm slices

1 tbsp sesame oil

salt and freshly ground black pepper

1. To make the roasted cabbage, preheat the oven to 200°C/400°F/Gas mark 6. Line a roasting tray with parchment paper.

2. Place the cabbage on the lined roasting tray, drizzle with the sesame oil and season with salt and pepper. Roast in the hot oven for 5–8 minutes until slightly charred. Remove from the oven and set aside to cool.

3. For the soup, bring the water to the boil in a saucepan then whisk in the miso. Reduce to a simmer, add the buckwheat noodles, prawns, beansprouts, smoked tofu, roasted cabbage and nori strips to the warm broth and cook for 5 minutes.

4. Pour into large bowls and garnish each with a few coriander leaves, chilli slices, sesame seeds and serve with a wedge of lime on the side.

GREEN CREAMY DETOX SOUP

If it's green and has the word detox in it then it must be good for you, right? Now I know there are so many examples of false marketing and advertising by using particular buzzwords but I can assure you that in this instance it is REALLY not the case. Just look at those ingredients and try to tell me otherwise! It's THA BOMB if you're feeling bloaty or under the weather.

SERVES 4-5

1 tbsp coconut oil
4 garlic cloves, peeled and cut in half
1 yellow onion (about 100g), cut in half then each half into thirds
375g broccoli (about 1 whole head of broccoli, stalks and all!), roughly chopped
1-2 courgettes (about 250g), cut into 2.5cm pieces
800ml water or unsalted vegetable stock
salt and freshly ground black pepper
100g baby spinach
25g coriander leaves and stems
4 tbsp pumpkin seeds
250ml unsweetened almond milk
drizzle of high-quality truffle oil (optional)

You will need a high-speed blender or food processor.

1. Heat the coconut oil in a casserole dish over a medium–low heat, add the garlic and onion and lightly sauté for 2–3 minutes until softened, but not coloured.

2. Add the broccoli and courgettes to the pan and pour in enough of the water or stock to cover. Add a pinch of salt and cook for 12–15 minutes until the vegetables are completely soft but not overcooked. Then throw in the baby spinach and coriander and stir well. Remove the pan from the heat, as you don't want overcooked vegetables and the residual heat will wilt the spinach and coriander.

3. Preheat the oven to 180°C/350°F/Gas mark 4.

4. Spread the pumpkin seeds out over a baking tray and toast in the hot oven for 5–7 minutes, turning every 2–3 minutes, until they are golden. Keep an eye on them as they can burn. Remove from the oven and set aside.

5. Place the vegetables in a high-speed blender with the almond milk and purée for 2–3 minutes until silky smooth. You might have to do this in batches. The key is to blend on high power until completely smooth, so start on low and then increase, otherwise the blender will spit. Season with salt and lots of pepper.

6. To serve, warm the soup gently, stirring frequently, until hot. Pour into bowls and garnish with the toasted pumpkin seeds and a drizzle of truffle oil, if you like.

MAMA'S CHICKEN CURRY

An ode to our mamas – thank you for giving us such a beautiful relationship with food, and thank you for giving us this recipe to share with you all today. CURRY IN A HURRY? Slightly sweet and slightly sour, this one's great for when you don't have much time and have a load of hungry people turning up for dinner.

SERVES 2–3

2 tbsp olive oil

1 yellow onion, roughly chopped

3 garlic cloves, peeled and crushed

1 green chilli, deseeded and finely chopped (optional)

15g piece ginger, peeled and finely chopped

1 low-sodium chicken stock cube

600g boneless skinless chicken breast fillet, cut into 2–3cm pieces

½ tbsp ground turmeric

2 tsp curry powder

1 tbsp gluten-free flour

10 cherry tomatoes

10g roughly chopped coriander, plus a few sprigs to garnish

juice of ½ lemon

TO SERVE

Freshly cooked brown rice (see page 100)

150g plain Greek yogurt

1. Heat a medium sauté pan over a medium heat and add the olive oil, onion, garlic, green chilli, if using, and ginger. Crush the chicken stock cube over and stir well so it breaks up. Cook for 5 minutes, or until the onion softens.

2. Add the chicken pieces and stir for about 5 minutes, or until the chicken starts to cook on the outside. Sprinkle in the turmeric and curry powder and stir well to make sure the spices coat all the ingredients. Sprinkle in the flour, again making sure that everything is coated, then add the tomatoes, coriander and lemon juice.

3. Pour in enough water just to barely cover the chicken mixture. Bring to a boil, then reduce the heat, cover and simmer for 20 minutes, or until the chicken is cooked and the water has almost evaporated.

4. Serve with brown rice, a dollop of Greek yogurt and some coriander sprigs sprinkled over the top.

LIGHT AND FRESH GAZPACHO

Soup does NOT have to be shelved during the summer. Let's get beach ready peoplezz! I present to you: Gazpacho and chilli toasted almonds – HOT DAYUMMM.

SERVES 4

1kg tomatoes, cut into quarters

1 green pepper, deseeded and roughly chopped

275g English cucumber, two-thirds roughly chopped

1 large garlic clove, peeled

50ml olive oil, plus extra for drizzling

30ml sherry vinegar

FOR THE CHILLI ALMONDS

60g flaked almonds, toasted

1 tbsp olive oil

¼ tsp smoked paprika

¼ tsp garlic granules

1 tsp salt

You will need a high-speed blender or food processor.

1. Blitz all the soup ingredients in a high-speed blender or food processor until completely smooth. Depending on the size of your blender you might have to do this in batches.

2. Strain the mixture through a sieve into a bowl so that it's completely smooth. This part is important to get a creamy smooth gazpacho. If you skip this step, expect there to be bits in your soup. Cover and chill for at least 1 hour before serving.

3. Preheat the oven to 180°C/350°F/Gas mark 4.

4. While the soup is chilling, combine all the ingredients for the chilli almonds in a small bowl, then spread them out on a non-stick baking tray and toast in the hot oven for 5–7 minutes, stirring every few minutes until golden. Keep an eye on the nuts to make sure they do not burn. Remove from the oven and set aside until ready to serve.

5. Serve the gazpacho in bowls with a sprinkle of the toasted chilli almonds and a drizzle of olive oil on top.

> Note: If you don't have sherry vinegar, apple cider vinegar, red wine vinegar or white vinegar will also work well.

HEARTY LENTIL SOUP

This one's a real filler-upper. It is probably one of the most satisfying recipes when it's the dead of winter, and deffo a meal on its own. There's something almost cosy about the whole recipe, it just makes me want to crawl up into a ball on the sofa and slurp this down while watching comfort TV.

SERVES 8

200g leeks, finely chopped
120g yellow onion, finely chopped
4 celery sticks (about 375g),
    finely chopped
200g carrots, finely chopped
3 garlic cloves, peeled and crushed
2 tbsp olive oil
2 tbsp tomato purée
2 thyme sprigs, leaves picked
250g green lentils
salt and freshly ground black
    pepper
2.25 litres water (or half
    vegetable stock and
    half water)
70g French beans, trimmed and
    cut into 1cm pieces
150g courgette, finely chopped
50g chard or kale, leaves only,
    finely chopped

TO GARNISH

small handful of chopped
    parsley
lemon wedges

1. Put the leeks, onion, celery, carrots and garlic into a casserole dish over a medium heat with the olive oil and coat well. Once the garlic is lightly browned and the vegetables have softened, about 5–7 minutes, add the tomato purée and thyme leaves and stir well. Add the lentils, a touch of salt and a few cracks of black pepper then stir until everything is well combined.

2. Pour in the water, bring to the boil then reduce the heat to a steady simmer and cook for about 35 minutes, or until the lentils are tender. Add the remaining vegetables and cook for a further 10 minutes. Season well and serve in bowls, garnished with chopped parsley and lemon wedges.

> Note: If you are preparing this soup in advance, don't add the French beans, courgette and chard or kale until you are ready to serve or they will go mushy. If you are making a large batch of soup to eat through the week, keep the lentil soup part separate from the French beans, courgette and chard or kale. Combine all the chopped veggies together and just add them in when you reheat your soup. This way the soup will still be fresh and crunchy.

BEEF CHILLI WITH LIME

HEY, HO CHILLI CHILLI BANG BANG! We opted for beef chunks rather than the standard mince, which in my opinion creates a much more filling, dynamic dish. It's an ideal scenario for chillin' at home in your pa-jay-jayz on a cold blustery night!! ***Warning*** You can adjust the amount of chilli to suit your taste in case you're not as crazy about spice as we are.

SERVES 4-6

500g beef shin or chuck steak,
   diced into 2cm cubes
salt and freshly ground black
   pepper
1 tbsp coconut oil
1 medium red onion
   (about 150g),
   peeled and diced
5 garlic cloves, peeled and
   crushed
150g piquillo peppers, sliced
1 red chilli, deseeded and
   chopped
½ tsp ground cinnamon
1½ tsp ground cumin
1 tsp smoked pimento pepper

2 tbsp lime juice (about 1 lime)
1 tbsp honey
1 tbsp cacao powder
500ml beef stock
30g coriander, roughly chopped
1 tsp chopped oregano
1 x 400g tin chopped tomatoes
1 x 400g tin kidney beans,
   drained and rinsed

TO SERVE

cumin brown rice (see page 164)
natural Greek yogurt or
   coconut yogurt
lime wedges
chopped fresh coriander

Recipe pictured overleaf.

1. Season the beef well. Heat a casserole dish over a high heat. When it is very hot add 1 tablespoon coconut oil and allow it to melt. Add the beef and fry for 5–6 minutes until it is nicely browned on all sides. When you first put the beef into the casserole, don't move it around, as you want to let it get some colour on one side before stirring it.

2. Once the beef is browned on all sides, add the red onion, garlic, piquillo peppers, chilli, cinnamon, cumin, smoked pimento pepper, lime juice, honey and cacao powder. Reduce the heat to medium and cook for 5–6 minutes, stirring well so that the onions and garlic don't burn, all the flavourings are incorporated into the beef and that they don't stick to the sides of the casserole.

3. Add the beef stock, coriander, oregano, chopped tomatoes, kidney beans and cook for 1½–2 hours. The whole house will smell incredible!

4. Serve the beef chilli with some cumin brown rice and topped with a dollop of Greek or coconut yogurt, a lime wedge and chopped coriander.

Variation: If you don't eat beef, you can use chicken, turkey, veal or other meat of your choice cut into cubes.

MAINS

ZUCCHINI FETTUCCINE

Spiralisationnnzzzz in the nationzzzz! This recipe is simple but please don't let this fool you – you are about to encounter a FLAVOUR EXPLOSION. It's guilt-free pasta, where every ingredient adds that little something extra. From the goat's cheese and roasted almonds to the sundried tomatoes, Mmm Mmm.

SERVES 4

1 tbsp coconut oil

300g Tenderstem broccoli, trimmed

4–5 courgettes

2 tbsp olive oil

130g sundried tomatoes, roughly chopped

80g edamame beans, podded

100g goat's cheese

50g roasted and salted almonds

salt and freshly ground black pepper

You will need a spiraliser or mandoline.

1. Heat a frying pan over a medium–high heat. When hot, add the coconut oil and allow it to melt. Add the broccoli and sauté for 4–5 minutes. Once you put the broccoli in the pan, don't move the pan, to allow one side of the broccoli to char. Once slightly charred, continue to cook until it is still al dente (with a bit of a bite) and set aside.

2. Push the courgettes through a spiraliser to make noodles or use a mandoline on the 'teeth' setting and put them into a large bowl. Add the oil and toss until the noodles are well coated. Add the sundried tomatoes with the charred broccoli, edamame beans, half of the goat's cheese and half of the almonds and mix well. Transfer to a large serving bowl and garnish with the remaining goat's cheese and roasted almonds.

> **Note:** You can serve this dish warm by adding all the ingredients, except the garnish, to a large frying pan on a medium heat for 3–4 minutes, stirring well to avoid the courgette wilting. Garnish with the goat's cheese and the roasted almonds.
>
> **Tip:** Want to change the game entirely? We implore you to toss in 200g of our homemade Almond Pesto (see page 185).

TOFU STIR-FRY

Whoever thinks tofu is boring, I suggest you indulge in this recipe so we can PROVE YOU WRONG. Tofu, for me, reminds me of the diet fads from the 90s and these days I have found a lot of people stay away from it, not just due to the soya content but also because the flavour can be rather bland, unless you know what to do with it. The marinade on this one is MAGIC and totally knocks this recipe out of the park – a good start to tofu 101.

SERVES 4

300g extra-firm tofu, drained
    and sliced into 1.5cm slices
1 tbsp honey
1 tbsp grated ginger
1 tbsp toasted sesame oil
50ml tamari
15g black sesame seeds
50g roasted almonds, sliced,
    to garnish

FOR THE STIR-FRIED VEGETABLES

2 tbsp coconut oil
30g piece ginger, peeled and
    finely sliced
200g shiitake mushrooms
1 head of broccoli (about 375g),
    separated into small florets
8 spring onions, diagonally sliced
200g asparagus spears, woody
    bits removed, cut on a bias
150g baby spinach, washed
50ml tamari
1 tbsp toasted sesame oil
1 tbsp lime juice

1. Put the tofu into a bowl and season with the honey, ginger, sesame oil and tamari. Cover and leave to marinate for at least 30 minutes.

2. When the tofu is ready to be cooked, heat a frying pan over a medium–high heat, remove the tofu from the marinade, reserving the marinade for later, and put the tofu in the pan. Sear for 3–4 minutes until it is golden on both sides. Reduce the heat to medium, add the reserved marinade to the tofu and allow to cook for another 2–3 minutes for the marinade to caramelise, then sprinkle the sesame seeds to coat. Set the pan aside.

3. For the stir-fry, heat a large pan over a high heat, melt the coconut oil and add the garlic, ginger, shiitake mushrooms, broccoli, spring onions and asparagus and cook for 4–5 minutes until they are almost cooked through. Then add in the spinach, tamari, sesame oil and lime juice and cook for an additional 2 minutes. The vegetables should remain tender and have a bit of a crunch.

4. Serve the stir-fried vegetables with the sticky tofu on top, garnished with sliced almonds.

RAW RAINBOW PAD THAI

YOU HAD ME AT PAD THAI AND RAINBOWS! Forget rice noodles, take it to the next level by putting beautifully coloured and vibrant veggies through your spiraliser, and there's no cooking involved! Is it just me, or is this brilliant?

SERVES 6-8

3 large courgettes, trimmed

3 sweet potatoes, peeled

½ white cabbage, quartered and
    finely chopped

½ red cabbage, quartered and
    finely chopped

2 red peppers, deseeded and
    finely sliced

1 yellow pepper, deseeded and
    finely sliced

handful of mint leaves, chopped

handful of coriander, leaves only,
    roughly chopped

3 beetroots, peeled

4 tbsp (100g) roasted cashews,
    chopped, to garnish

FOR THE PAD THAI DRESSING

150g raw cashew nuts

100ml white wine vinegar

100ml soy sauce

40ml lemon juice

5 tbsp honey

2½ tsp salt

2 garlic cloves, peeled and
    finely diced

12g piece of ginger, peeled and
    finely diced

½ whole red chilli, chopped
    into chunks

110ml water

1. To make the dressing, mix all the ingredients together in a saucepan and simmer over a medium heat for 10 minutes. This will soften the cashews. Transfer the mixture to a blender and blitz until super-smooth. Set aside.

2. Push the courgettes through a spiraliser, then push the sweet potatoes through the spiraliser. You can use the 'teeth' setting on the mandoline if you don't have a spiraliser. Slice the cabbage using the flat blade of a mandoline or chop it very thinly with a knife.

3. Mix all the ingredients, except for the beetroot, together in a large bowl.

4. To finish, push the beetroot through the spiraliser – but keep it separate until you are ready to serve, otherwise the beetroot's colour will bleed into everything else. When ready to serve, place the salad in a bowl, drizzle the dressing over and toss it well. Garnish with the roasted cashews.

> You will need a high-speed blender for the dressing and a spiraliser or mandoline for the veg.

AUBERGINE PASTA SALAD

Both our boyfriends are human rubbish disposals (no offence, boys) so **FORGET ABOUT LEFTOVERS.** I even saw one of them peering into a bowl of raw marinating chicken the other day, I meaaannn... The success of this dish came from finding the remnants of an empty bowl still left in the fridge (we obviously know who to blame) but it's a serious all-round winner. It's best served warm or at room temperature for lunch or as an accompaniment.

SERVES 4-5

400g aubergine
olive oil, for greasing
100g cherry tomatoes
150g gluten-free fusilli
1 tbsp tahini
1 tbsp balsamic vinegar
100g rocket
1 tbsp chopped basil
salt and freshly ground
    black pepper

> Note: This is a great recipe to eat warm or at room temperature as a pasta salad. Depending on the type of gluten-free fusilli, some pasta can get slightly hard when chilled, so you will need to reheat it slightly or let it come back to room temperature before serving the dish.

1. Preheat the oven to 220°C/425°F/Gas mark 7 and lightly grease a baking tray. Fill a large casserole dish with water and a pinch of salt and bring to the boil.

2. Start by roasting the aubergine, by cutting it in half and seasoning with salt and pepper and a drizzle of olive oil, making sure the flesh is well coated. Turn the aubergine flesh side down on the tray and roast in the oven for 20–30 minutes, depending on its thickness. You want to roast until the flesh is completely soft.

3. Cut the tomatoes in half, season with salt and pepper and lightly toss with a splash of olive oil. Place them in a corner of the baking tray next to the aubergine for 5–7 minutes, just enough time for them to slightly soften. Remove just the tomatoes and allow them to cool while the aubergine continues to cook.

4. You want to time this step well so the pasta is warm when the aubergine is ready. Cook the fusilli according to the packet instructions. Drain, drizzle with olive oil and set aside.

5. When the aubergine is soft, remove from the oven and scoop the flesh into a large bowl. Add the tahini and balsamic vinegar and mix to combine. Add the cooked fusilli, wilted tomatoes, rocket and basil, then season with salt and pepper and mix together. Serve.

BUTTERNUT GNOCCHI

Gnocchi is the epitome of cosiness. Nothing beats a good gnocchi with some homemade marinara sauce. You might be thinking that using butternut squash is slightly out of the ordinary, but these gnocchi create snuggly little drops of goodness that melt in your mouth. What can be better for a movie night at home? AM I RIGHT?

SERVES 4

1 large butternut squash
    (about 1.2kg)
2 tbsp olive oil
260g gluten-free flour, plus
    extra for dusting
2 eggs
1 tbsp dried oregano
2 tbsp nutritional yeast flakes
1 tbsp sea salt
1 quantity Tomato Sauce
    (see page 134), to serve
Parmesan or nutritional yeast
    flakes, to serve

A potato ricer is recommended.

1. Preheat the oven 200°C/400°F/Gas mark 6.

2. Cut the butternut squash in half. Lightly oil the flesh with 1 tablespoon of the oil and place flesh-side down on a non-stick baking tray. Roast in the oven for about 30 minutes or until the flesh is soft. Remove from the oven and scrape out the flesh with a spoon then pass it through a potato ricer or mash with the back of a fork. Discard the skin.

3. Put the mashed butternut squash in a large bowl with the remaining ingredients and mix together with your hands or a wooden spoon.

4. Dust the work surface lightly with flour, divide the squash mixture into tennis ball-sized pieces and roll into a thin log, depending on the thickness you would like. Using a knife, cut off the first end, which will be uneven, and discard and then cut off 2–3cm pieces. Use the tines of a fork to press down lightly on the top of each piece.

5. Once you have made all your gnocchi, heat the remaining oil in a large pan over a medium heat. Add the gnocchi, you don't want to overcrowd the pan so you may need to do this in 2 batches, and cook the gnocchi for 5–6 minutes, tossing them around so they don't burn. Once cooked, add the Tomato Sauce and heat for a few minutes until it is warmed through.

6. Serve with Parmesan or yeast flakes.

ROASTED TOMATO AND COD

I always found it hard to pinpoint an easy go-to fish dish to make at home, until we came up with this one. It's very simple. The seasoning on the roasted tomatoes – the sumac and saffron – are very much considered as the fundamentals of Persian cuisine, combined with the pan-fried cod... YUMMMAAAYYY. Sumac in particular is not often used in the West; just to shed some light on the flavour itself, it produces a somewhat 'lemony' taste. I would also urge you to try sprinkling some on salads and meat to add some of that delicious deep zesty 'flavaaaa'.

½ tsp saffron threads
4 vine tomatoes, cut into
    quarters
1 tbsp olive oil
1 tsp coconut sugar
sea salt
1 tsp sumac
¼ tsp chilli powder
1 tbsp sherry or red
    wine vinegar

4 x 125g cod fillets,
    skin on
salt and freshly ground
    black pepper
1 tbsp olive oil
1 tbsp white wine (optional)
lime wedges, to serve

Cauliflower rice (see
    page 162)

Preheat the oven 200°C/400°F/Gas mark 6.

Add the saffron threads to a small bowl filled with boiling water and leave to infuse for 5 minutes.

In a bowl, toss the tomatoes with the oil, saffron water, sugar, salt, spices and vinegar, then put it all into a roasting tray and bake in the hot oven for 30 minutes, turning twice, or until caramelised. Leave to cool and the juices should start to become sticky.

Meanwhile, season the fish fillets on both sides with salt and pepper. Heat a pan over a high heat, add the olive oil and allow it to melt. Put the cod skin-side down in the pan and cook for 4–5 minutes, or until the skin is crispy. Flip over and cook for a further 1–2 minutes, adding the wine, if using, and basting the fish with (use a spoon to pour the sauce back over the fish to keep it moist).

Put some Cauliflower rice on a plate, place the fish on top and lay 3–4 pieces of tomato on the fish. Dress with the juice of the roasted tomatoes and serve with a lime wedge.

ZUCCHINI MARINARA WITH SPICY PRAWNS

We are huge courgette fans here at The Good Life, especially when they are made into ZOODLES, OODLES, NOOOODLESSSSSS – sorry, I get overexcited. Turn the heat up with these spicy prawns – it's always nice to see the diversity in flavour you can create by adding that kick of chilli.

SERVES 4

FOR THE TOMATO SAUCE

3 garlic cloves, peeled and
    crushed or finely chopped
4 tbsp extra virgin
    olive oil
400g plum tomatoes,
    finely chopped
300g cherry tomatoes, halved
¼ fresh red chilli, deseeded
    and finely chopped
2 tbsp tomato purée
a pinch of salt
½ tbsp balsamic vinegar
1 tbsp chopped flat-leaf parsley

FOR THE ONION OIL

¼ yellow onion, peeled and
    finely chopped
2–3 tbsp extra-virgin
    olive oil

1. To make the onion oil, put the onion into a bowl, add the olive oil and make sure it is all well combined. Leave to stand at room temperate to allow all the flavours to absorb.

2. Start preparing the tomato sauce. Put the garlic into a saucepan, add the olive oil and place over a low heat. Cook the garlic for 3–4 minutes, or until it is lightly golden, not burnt. Then add all the tomatoes, the chilli, tomato purée, salt and balsamic vinegar. Increase the heat to medium and cook for 20 minutes to allow the tomatoes to soften and melt down. Once the tomatoes have softened, add the chopped parsley and onion-oil and continue cooking for 20 minutes to allow the onion oil flavour to infuse into the tomatoes. Keep the sauce warm for serving.

3. For the spicy prawns, combine all the dry ingredients in a bowl, add the olive oil and mix well. Dry the prawns well with kitchen paper and then toss in the spicy oil until they are coated.

4. Push the courgettes through a spiraliser or use a mandoline. Transfer the strands to a bowl and set aside.

FOR THE SPICY PRAWNS

¼ tsp chilli powder
2 tsp garlic powder
a pinch of salt
½ tsp ground black pepper
1 tbsp olive oil
250–300g king prawns, peeled
and deveined

TO SERVE

5 courgettes
150–200g Tenderstem broccoli,
cut into 2.5cm pieces
large pinch of chopped basil,
to garnish

You will need a spiraliser or
mandoline.

Recipe pictured overleaf.

5. Heat a large frying pan over a medium heat. Add the prawns and broccoli pieces and sauté for 3–5 minutes, or until the prawns turn pink and are cooked.

6. In a large bowl, combine the courgette noodles with the warm tomato sauce until fully coated.

7. Serve the courgette noodles and tomato sauce in a large pasta bowl with the prawns and broccoli scattered over the top, garnished with basil.

Tip: When cutting tomatoes, a serrated paring knife works best.

STICKY CHICKEN

Chicken tastes so good it makes me wanna slap yo Mamaaa! I think our dearest photographer Toby found this dish the most difficult to shoot as I was trying to stuff it into my mouth 30 seconds after it was ready. Aside from the salivating factor, this recipe is relatively quick and requires little prep. Also, I truly believe the thigh isn't given enough street cred these days. GIMME SOME OF THAT STICKY ICKAAYYYY.

SERVES 4

500g chicken thighs (about
    4 thighs)
1 tbsp olive oil
300ml chicken stock
4 garlic cloves, peeled and crushed
100g salad onions, finely
    chopped
3 tbsp honey
60ml rice vinegar
40g piece of ginger, peeled
    and cut into thin batons
60ml tamari
salt and freshly ground
    black pepper
sautéed broccoli, to serve

1. Start by seasoning the skin of the chicken thighs with salt and pepper.

2. Heat a flameproof casserole dish over a high heat. When hot, add the olive oil and the chicken, skin-side down, and cook for 8–10 minutes, or until the skin is golden. If the oil is spitting, reduce the heat slightly. Once the skin is golden, flip it over and cook flesh-side down for 3–4 minutes. Remove the chicken from the dish and put on a plate.

3. Strain the fat from the pan, still leaving all the brown bits on the bottom and put the casserole dish back over a high heat. Add in the chicken stock, garlic, half of the salad onions, honey, rice vinegar, ginger and tamari and allow it to reduce by half, this will take about 15 minutes. Then return the chicken thighs to the pan, skin side up.

4. Cook for 25–30 minutes; keep coating the chicken with the sauce. The sauce should reduce to a level where it coats the back of a spoon.

5. Garnish with the remaining salad onions and serve with some sautéed broccoli.

SWEET POTATO PASTA WITH CHICKEN BOLOGNESE

Your not-so-standard Spag Bol! In an effort to keep things **FRAYSH** and **LIGHT**, this is something you definitely need to experience. Make sure you don't overcook the sweet potato pasta, so it doesn't turn mushy – it definitely needs a little bite to it to get that al dente feelingzzz.

SERVES 4-6

1 tbsp coconut oil

1 yellow onion, peeled and chopped

3 garlic cloves, peeled and finely chopped

1 thumb of ginger, peeled and finely chopped

¼ tsp chilli powder

400g chicken mince

2 tbsp white wine

1 x 400g tin chopped tomatoes

10g parsley, roughly chopped

10g basil, roughly chopped

4–6 large sweet potatoes

a sprinkle of grated Parmesan or nutritional yeast flakes

You will need a spiraliser or a mandoline.

1. Heat the coconut oil in a large saucepan over a low heat. Add the onion, garlic, ginger and chilli and cook slowly for 7–8 minutes until the onion is soft and translucent. Add the chicken mince and use a wooden spoon to break up the meat into small pieces so it gets nicely browned. Once browned, add the wine, chopped tomatoes and half the herbs and stir with the wooden spoon to remove any crispy bits from the base of the pan, then cook on medium–low heat for 20 minutes.

2. Peel the sweet potatoes and push through a spiraliser on the thin noodle setting or use a mandoline.

3. Once your bolognese is ready, add the spiralised sweet potato to your pan and stir well. The noodles should be nicely coated in sauce. Warm them in the sauce for 3–5 minutes to slightly soften.

4. Transfer to a large bowl and garnish with the remaining herbs and grated Parmesan or nutritional yeast flakes.

GREEN CHICKEN MEATBALLS

These are cheerful, delicious and an easaayyy breezayyy way to feed a crowd. I'll have these bad boys on pretty much anything these days, or even just on their own. In a sandwich, on a salad, in a bowl with rice... they are the go-to protein, and the herb combo makes the insides a deep greeny colour, which I enjoy... simply because there needs to be **MORE GREEN** food in this world!

SERVES 4/
MAKES ABOUT 20 MEATBALLS

75g white button mushrooms

½ medium yellow onion
    (about 60g), peeled

1 egg

20g basil, including stems

20g parsley, including stems

10g coriander

500g white chicken mince

20g gluten-free breadcrumbs

1 tsp salt

¼ tsp freshly ground black
    pepper

1 tbsp olive oil

TO SERVE

Brown rice (see page 100)

wilted chopped spinach

1 quantity Tomato Sauce (optional),
    (see page 134)

Greek yogurt

You will need a food processor.

1. Put the mushrooms and onion into the food processor and blitz until they are really small pieces, then put them into a large bowl.

2. Add the egg, basil, parsley and coriander into the food processor and blitz until it is a smooth, green and has a paste-like consistency. Add the mixture to the mushroom and onions, then add the chicken mince and breadcrumbs and season with the salt and pepper. Mix well with your hands until the mixture is fully combined. It should be bright green. This is a soft meatball mixture so you won't be able to roll them perfectly. Using damp, clean hands, split the mixture into about 20 golf-ball-sized meatballs, weighing 40–50g each.

3. Heat the olive oil in a large frying pan over a medium heat and fry the meatballs, in batches if necessary, for 10–12 minutes or until brown on all sides.

4. Serve the meatballs with cooked brown rice, wilted spinach, the Tomato sauce, if using, and a dollop of Greek yogurt.

SAFFRON CHICKEN SKEWERS

Joojeh Kabob – is what we call this back in the old country, but we've tweaked it a bit to make it fit our GOOD LIFE VIBINGZZZ. The key to this dish is the marinade – the longer the marinating period the more intense the flavours will be. So this goes back to our philosophy of prepping the day before... get your prep on. Your end result should be a beautiful, fragrant, bright yellow skewer of golden lean and juicy chicken breast.

SERVES 4

a pinch of saffron threads
    (about 10 threads)
2 tbsp boiling water
½ large white onion (about
    100g), peeled and grated
2 tbsp lemon juice
50g natural Greek yogurt
salt and freshly ground black
    pepper
500g skinless and boneless
    chicken breast, cut into
    3cm cubes

TO SERVE

Brown barberry rice (see
    page 165)
Cucumber yogurt (see
    page 190)

Recipe pictured overleaf.

1. Soak the saffron in the boiling water for 10 minutes.

2. Put the onion, lemon juice, saffron and soaking water, yogurt, salt and pepper into a large bowl and combine well. Add the chicken cubes and toss until the chicken is coated all over. Cover the bowl with clingfilm and chill in the fridge for 1 hour, or overnight.

3. If you can't get hold of metal skewers and are using wooden ones, soak them in a bowl of water for 30 minutes before using to ensure the wood does not burn.

4. Thread the marinated chicken onto several skewers, about 125g of chicken per skewer, and grill on a preheated griddle pan for 5–6 minutes on each side. The chicken should be a nice brown colour on each side.

5. Serve the skewers over the Brown barberry rice with Cucumber yogurt.

SPRINGTIME PENNE

This is a **DEE-LISH**, heartwarming dinner for all the family to enjoy. Light and crunchy is the beauty of this dish, and make sure you make that **SAWCE EXTRA SAWWWCEEEEYYYY.**

SERVES 4

olive oil, for cooking
100g shallots, peeled and cut into long very thin slices
2 garlic cloves, peeled and crushed or very finely chopped
1 tsp dried red chilli flakes
400g asparagus, woody stems trimmed and cut on the diagonal into 2.5cm pieces
250g cherry tomatoes, halved
250g fresh or frozen peas
400g gluten-free penne
30g rocket, roughly chopped
10g basil, leaves only, roughly chopped
Parmesan or nutritional yeast flakes, for serving
salt and freshly ground black pepper

1. Bring a large saucepan of salted water to the boil over a high heat.

2. Meanwhile, heat a generous amount of olive oil in a separate pan over a medium heat. Add the shallots, garlic and red chilli flakes and cook for about 2–3 minutes, or until they start to melt and become translucent. You don't want the shallots to burn or have colour. Add the asparagus, tomatoes and peas and continue cooking for 7–8 minutes until the veggies are cooked through but still have a crunch.

3. Once the water is boiling in the saucepan add the pasta. It is important to slightly undercook the pasta by about 2 minutes in this recipe.

4. Once the pasta is ready, remove about 60ml water with a ladle and set aside, then strain the pasta straight away and add it to the vegetables with the reserved pasta water. Allow the water to absorb into the pasta and finish cooking, season with salt and pepper, then add the rocket and basil.

5. Serve with a little Parmesean or a sprinkle of nutritional yeast flakes if you want to keep it dairy-free.

> Tip: Gluten-free pasta likes to stick together, so make sure to stir occasionally. Don't add olive oil to the pasta water, as this causes the oil to coat the pasta when you drain it, which will inhibit it from absorbing the sauce!

BAKED SQUA-GHETTI

I know what you're wondering, how on this good earth are you going to turn squash into 'spaghetti'? No gadgets required, so **READ ON** to find out! This is an interesting way to create a baked-style pasta without actually having to use pasta. Squash made into spaghetti and baked in the oven with homemade marinara and mozzarella... is your mouth watering yet?

SERVES 4

1 tbsp olive oil
2 spaghetti squash, cut in half
    lengthways and deseeded
salt and freshly ground black
    pepper
1 quantity Tomato Sauce
    (see page 134)
1 large mozzarella ball,
    sliced or 4 tbsp nutritional
    yeast flakes
10 basil leaves, chopped
1 tbsp chilli flakes

SALAD, TO SERVE

A few handfuls of any green
    salad leaves
2–3 tbsp olive oil
1 tbsp lemon juice
salt and freshly ground
    black pepper

1. Preheat the oven to 200°C/400°F/Gas mark 6.

2. Rub the olive oil over the cut sides of both squash halves and sprinkle generously with salt and pepper. Place the squash, cut-side down, on a non-stick baking sheet and bake in the hot oven for about 30–35 minutes until the squash is just tender enough to scrape into strands with a fork. You don't want it to be mushy. Remove the squash from the oven and allow to cool for a few minutes until you can touch the outside shell. Hold the shell with one hand and scrape the insides into strands or 'spaghetti' lightly with a fork, but keeping it inside the squash.

3. If you are serving the squash with the mozzarella, then after scraping the squash add about 4–6 tablespoons of the tomato sauce onto the squash and add a layer of mozzarella. Return the squash to the oven for 5–6 minutes to allow it to melt, then garnish with the basil and chilli flakes. If you are making the recipe without the cheese just garnish with the nutritional yeast, basil and chilli and enjoy it immediately.

4. Serve with the green salad leaves and a drizzle of olive oil and lemon juice and a little seasoning.

CHICKEN LETTUCE BURGER

In other words, a juicy minced chicken and herb patty wrapped in crunchy iceberg lettuce is EXCELLENT for when you want to keep the old carb count down. Come on, how good does that look?

SERVES 5

1 courgette

700g chicken mince (mixture of white and dark meat)

2 garlic cloves, peeled and crushed

½ tsp dried red chilli flakes

30g edamame beans, podded

2 tbsp chopped mint

2 tbsp chopped tarragon

2 tbsp chopped parsley

2 tbsp chopped coriander

1 egg

5 tsp olive oil, for frying

TO SERVE

1 head of iceberg lettuce, peel off the outer leaves one by one to make the bun

5 tbsp Dijon mustard

1–2 large beef tomato, sliced

1 red onion, peeled and thinly sliced

Beetroot Slaw (see page 158), to serve

Recipe pictured overleaf.

1. To make the burgers, grate the courgette into a bowl. Add all the remaining ingredients except the oil and mix together well. Using clean, damp hands, form the mixture into 5 patties.

2. Heat the oil in a large frying pan over a medium heat and fry the patties in batches, if necessary, for 4–5 minutes on each side or until golden brown.

3. Peel the outer leaves off the lettuce one by one. Place on a plate and place a burger on top. Load up with 1 tablespoon Dijon mustard, beef tomato slices and red onion and serve with a side of Beetroot Slaw.

DOWNTOWN SWEET PO'TATTER

SPUDDD LIFEEE. Oh man, this is the real deal right here, jacket potatoes are popular with everybody. Sweet potato and turkey combos get me all riled up and ready to conquer the world. I feel like not many people in the UK turn to turkey, and I have yet to pinpoint why, but they should!

SERVES 4-6

4–6 sweet potatoes (about 200–250g each)

2 tbsp olive oil

250g white onion (about 1½ onions), sliced into half moons

3 garlic cloves, peeled and chopped

500g minced turkey

2 tsp cumin seeds

½ tsp smoked paprika, plus extra for serving

35g green pitted olives, sliced into rounds

½ x 400g tin chopped tomatoes

50g fresh or frozen peas

juice of 1 lime

200g red pepper (about 1 pepper), deseeded and chopped into 2cm cubes

1 medium or 2 small ripe avocados

5g coriander, roughly torn, to garnish

4–6 tbsp Greek yogurt, to serve

1. Preheat the oven to 200°C/220°F/Gas mark 6. Pierce each sweet potato a few times, then wrap in foil. Roast in the oven for 45 minutes, or until soft when pierced with a knife.

2. Meanwhile, start preparing the filling. Heat half the oil in a non-stick frying pan over a medium-low heat. Add the onion and garlic and cook for 10 minutes, or until the onion softens and turns translucent.

3. Add the turkey, turn the heat to high and fry for 10 minutes, stirring occasionally, until the turkey is browned. Add the cumin, smoked paprika, olives, crushed tomatoes, peas, lime juice and red pepper and simmer for 7–8 minutes, then cover and keep over an extra-low heat until ready to serve.

4. Peel and stone the avocados. Scoop the flesh into a bowl and mash with a fork. Set aside.

5. Remove the sweet potatoes from the oven, make an incision down the centre and open it wide enough to stuff. Add about a quarter of the turkey mixture and top with the avocado, coriander, a dusting of smoked paprika and a dollop of Greek yogurt.

Tip: If you can't find minced turkey, any type of lean minced meat will work well here.

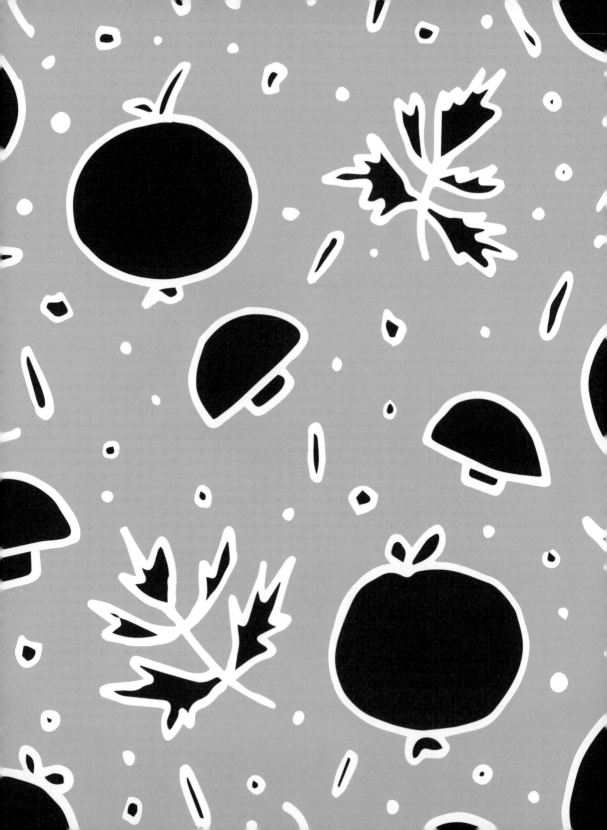

SIDES

SUMMERY TOMATO AND HERB SALAD

This salad is great to eat with any simple grilled steak or fish or served as a side dish at a barbecue. SO DAM FRAICHE!

SERVES 4

½ small shallot, finely chopped

1 tbsp sherry vinegar

½ tsp dried oregano

5 tbsp olive oil

70g capers, drained

500g ripe cherry tomatoes, cut in half

15g basil leaves, roughly chopped

30g flat leaf parsley, roughly chopped

75g feta cheese, crumbled

salt and freshly ground black pepper

1. In a mixing bowl, combine the chopped shallot, sherry vinegar, dried oregano and 4 tablespoons of the olive oil, then cover and allow everything to infuse with each other while you prepare the rest of the salad.

2. Heat the remaining 1 tablespoon olive oil over a medium heat in a small frying pan, add the drained capers and fry for 1–2 minutes until crispy. Be careful as they will splatter. Remove from the heat and set aside.

3. Add the tomatoes, basil, parsley and capers to the bowl with the shallot and sherry vinegar dressing and toss well. Season very lightly with salt and generously with freshly ground pepper – the feta and capers are both quite salty already. Top with the crumbled feta and serve.

FENNEL AND PARMESAN SIDE SALAD

Ever wondered what to serve your guests instead of your standard green salad? Let's think outside the box here PEOPLEZZZ. This salad is amazing with any simple fish dish. You don't need too much Parmesan – a little goes a loooong way.

SERVES 6-8

2 medium fennel bulbs (about 700g), trimmed
50g Parmesan, coarsely grated
75g walnuts, roughly chopped
1 tbsp chopped parsley
juice of 2 lemons
olive oil, for coating
salt and freshly ground black pepper

You will need a mandoline.

1. Cut the fennel in half and shave into 2mm vertical slices on a mandoline. If you don't have a mandoline, then cut into extremely thin slices with a knife. Put into a large bowl.

2. Add the remaining ingredients to the bowl, using just enough olive oil to lightly coat the fennel leaves. Season well with salt and pepper and serve.

BEETROOT SLAW

This side brings a beautiful, ENERGETIC pop of colour to any dish. I'm always trying to find new ways of presenting a classic side, and switching up the ingredients is a great way of achieving some variation and originality.

SERVES 2-3

200g beetroot, peeled and cut
    into matchsticks or use the wide
    'teeth' setting of a mandoline
2 carrots (about 75g), peeled
    and cut into matchsticks or use
    the wide 'teeth' setting of a
    mandoline
10g finely chopped dill
15g finely chopped mint leaves
100g red cabbage, finely
    shredded
100g white cabbage, finely
    shredded
1 tbsp red wine vinegar
10g honey
250g organic mayonnaise,
    veganaise or natural Greek
    yogurt
salt and freshly ground black
    pepper

A mandoline is recommended.

1. To make the slaw, put all the ingredients into a large bowl, season to taste and gently stir together until well mixed.

2. Cover and keep in the fridge until needed.

MIXED MUSHROOMS

We **LOVE SHROOOOMSS.** This is awesome as a side dish, or my personal fave as an open-face shroom sandwichhhhh. Just put the shrooms on top of a slice of toasted sourdough, sprinkle a bit of Parmesan over the top – **ET VOILA!**

SERVES 4

100g enoki mushrooms

100g shimeji (white or brown beech) mushrooms

200g shiitake mushrooms

200g trumpet mushrooms

1 tbsp olive oil

2 large garlic cloves, peeled and crushed

50ml white wine

1 tsp arrowroot mixed with 3 tbsp water

6 sage leaves, chopped

salt and freshly ground black pepper

1. Start by preparing and cleaning the mushrooms. I tend not to wash mushrooms, just use some kitchen paper to rub off any dirt. Enoki and shimeji (beech) mushrooms are easy to prepare as they are attached with a central stem at the bottom, which needs to be removed and discarded. Shiitake mushrooms have a very leathery stem, which needs to be snapped off at the base then the mushrooms cut in half. Trumpet mushrooms just need to be cut into 2–3mm slices.

2. Heat the oil in a non-stick pan over a medium–high heat. When hot, add the mushrooms and crushed garlic and cook for 10–12 minutes, stirring regularly until the mushrooms are browned and all the liquid released from the mushrooms has been absorbed.

3. Pour the wine into the pan and cook for 2 minutes, or until the wine has been completely absorbed. Add the arrowroot mixture and stir well then immediately remove from the heat and add the chopped sage. Season well with salt and pepper and serve.

Note: You will need 600g of mixed mushrooms for this dish. I like to use a mix of enoki, shimeji (white or brown beech), shiitake and trumpet mushrooms, but if you can't find these then use whatever you can find or what's in season.

EDAMAME AND PEA SLAW

How boring is coleslaw? And how can you make it un-boring? I know... ADD SOME PEASSSSS AND EDAMAMEEEEE! This is an amazing side dish for nearly anything I can think of.

SERVES 4-6

2 tbsp Dijon mustard

1 tbsp honey

2 tbsp Greek yogurt

2 tbsp apple cider vinegar

6 tbsp olive oil

salt and freshly ground black pepper

½ red cabbage

50g edamame beans, podded

20g pea shoots

1. Start by making the dressing in a large bowl. Combine the mustard, honey, Greek yogurt, apple cider vinegar, olive oil and salt and pepper and whisk well until the dressing has become thick.

2. Finely chop the red cabbage. Add the chopped cabbage to the bowl of dressing and add in the edamame beans and pea shoots. Stir well and enjoy.

QUINOA

Little beads of carby goodness, the preferable wheat-free substitute that's taking the nation by storm. You can incorporate this into any dish, ranging from salads, lunch, mains – even breakfast options.

MAKES 600G COOKED QUINOA/ SERVES 2-3

300g quinoa

2 pinches of sea salt

Tip: Rule of thumb – quinoa doubles in volume once cooked.

1. Put the quinoa in a pan and pour over twice the volume of water (so 600ml), add the salt and bring to the boil.

2. Reduce the heat and simmer for 15 minutes, uncovered. The quinoa is cooked once tender and you can see the 'tails'. Don't overcook, as it will continue to cook whilst cooling. Remove from the heat and cover for 5 minutes to cool. Fluff with a fork and leave to cool.

CAULIFLOWER RICE

Cauliflower rice, oh wow! This is the perfect replacement for carbs in any meal. Not feeling like a heavy lunch or dinner? Just replace the carb element, be it rice, quinoa or spelt, with this recipe.

SERVES 4

1½–2 heads of cauliflower

3 tbsp coriander, finely chopped

3 tbsp flat or curly parsley, finely chopped

3 tbsp mint leaves, finely chopped

3 tbsp tarragon, finely chopped

1 tsp nigella seeds

salt and freshly ground black pepper

3 tbsp water

A food processor or box grater is recommended.

1. Remove the outer leaves of the cauliflower and chop the cauliflower into 3cm pieces. You can use the inner stalk as well, if you like. Put in a food processor and pulse until it is a couscous-like consistency. If you don't have a food processor, you can finely chop the cauliflower with a knife or use a box grater. In a bowl, combine the cauliflower rice with the chopped herbs, nigella seeds and season well with salt and pepper.

2. Heat a medium saucepan over a medium–low heat, add the cauliflower rice mixture and 3 tablespoons of water and cover for 5 minutes to allow it to steam and enjoy! Serve with the Roasted Tomato and Cod (see page 132).

> Variation: You can eat this raw.

BROWN RICE

AKA whole grain rice, chewier in consistency than the regular white rice. It is not a different type of rice, just the same as white rice before it has been put through certain processes. There has been a lot of controversy lately as to whether or not white rice is better than brown rice, so I am not going to delve into that side of things. JUST ENJOY IT!

SERVES 2-3

350g short-grain brown rice
700ml water
2 vegetable stock cubes
a generous pinch of salt

1. Put the rice into a large saucepan, add the water to cover and crumble in the stock cubes with a generous pinch of salt. Bring to the boil.

2. Cover, reduce the heat and simmer for about 30 minutes, or until the rice is tender.

3. Drain, add back to the pan and cover for 5 minutes to let the residual water absorb..

CUMIN BROWN RICE

You get the chewy consistency from the brown rice with an earthy warm cumin aroma, enhancing the flavour of many meals which you feel need that extra OOF FACTOR.

SERVES 4

350g brown basmati rice
1 tbsp ground cumin
700ml water

1. Put the rice and ground cumin into a medium saucepan. Give it a good stir so the cumin coats the rice grains and they slightly toast.

2. Add the water, bring to the boil, lower the heat to a simmer and cook for 30 minutes, or until the rice is tender.

3. Drain, add back to the pan and cover for 5 minutes to let the residual water absorb.

BROWN BARBERRY RICE

This rice dish is truly a gem of the Middle East. Barberries are very native to Iranian cooking and have most recently been categorised as a superfood (YEH MAN!) The taste is very similar to a dried cranberry, so combined with the saffron and coconut sugar, you get this sweet and sour aroma in every mouthful. That's it, I'm making this for dinner tonight!

SERVES 4

200g brown basmati rice
salt
400ml water (for the rice)
a pinch of saffron threads
    (about 10 threads)
3 tbsp boiling water (for the saffron)
50g barberries
½ tbsp organic butter
1 tsp coconut sugar or unrefined
    cane sugar
2 tbsp water (for the barberries)

1. In a large saucepan, bring the rice, a generous pinch or two of salt and the 400ml water to the boil. Once boiling, reduce the heat to medium–low and cook for 25–30 minutes, until the rice is tender. Drain and set aside.

2. Meanwhile, soak the saffron threads in the boiling water for 10 minutes. Rinse the barberries in a colander to remove any impurities.

3. Put the barberries into a small pan with the butter, sugar and the water and allow them to warm up for 5 minutes over a very low heat, stirring constantly. Remove from the heat and set aside. When the rice is ready, drain, then add the barberries and saffron water and lightly toss until the rice is coated. Be gentle when mixing the rice otherwise the grains will stick together. Enjoy with the Saffron chicken skewers (see page 143).

Tip: Wash and sift the barberries before using as the packet can contain small stones.

DRESSINGS AND DIPS

BEETROOT DIP

I'm nearly almost certain that the last thing you would think to do with a sad, lonely beetroot sitting in your fridge is to make it into a dip. The various spices really bring out the sweetness in the beetroot and creates an enchanting Middle Eastern aroma, which is perfect for a quick chips 'n' dip sesh. **TURN UP THE BEET!**

SERVES 8-10

750g beetroot, unpeeled
½ tbsp ground cumin
½ tbsp ground coriander
½ tbsp za'atar, plus extra
 for garnish
½ tbsp harissa paste
1 garlic clove, peeled
2 Medjool dates, pitted
1¼ tbsp olive oil
salt and freshly ground
 black pepper

You will need a food processor.

1. Preheat the oven to 175°C/347°F/Gas mark 4.

2. Put the whole beetroot on a baking tray and cover with foil. Cook in the oven for about 45 minutes, depending on size, or until the beetroot is completely soft when you pierce it with a knife. The beetroot should be soft but not mushy. Remove the beetroot from the oven and leave to cool slightly, then peel off the skin. This should be easy to do with your hands or a small knife. Rough chop the beetroot and set aside.

3. Put all the spices, garlic and dates into a food processor and blitz until crumbled. Then add the beetroot and olive oil and pulse until it is a dip-like consistency but still slightly chunky. Transfer to a bowl and set aside until ready to eat. Garnish with some za'atar.

4. Serve with Everything crackers (see page 201) or toasted pita bread.

PARSNIP AND BUTTER BEAN DIP

Let's get real for a quick, **HOT** minute – parsnip and beans aren't usually the attraction of any recipe **BUT** (and if you haven't noticed throughout this book, there will always be a but) we like to take the unusual and turn it into the **DEEEEE-LICIOUS**. It is best served with some crudités (see page 176) or crispbread.

SERVES 4

250g parsnips, peeled and cut into chunks

2 garlic cloves, peeled

1/2 tbsp dried thyme

250g tin butter beans, drained

1 tbsp olive oil, plus extra to garnish

1/2 tbsp lemon juice

salt and freshly ground black pepper

1. Boil the parsnips and the whole garlic cloves in a pan of boiling water for 15 minutes, or until soft all the way through. Check that they are soft by piercing with a knife. Drain and leave to cool.

2. Place the cooled parsnips and garlic in a food processor with the remaining ingredients and blitz until smooth. Season well with salt and pepper. Transfer the dip to a bowl and serve immediately. Garnish with a drizzle of olive oil and a crack of black pepper.

SWEET POTATO DIP

This, MY GOOD (LIFE) PEOPLEZZZZ, is the dip of all dips. It's definitely one of my favourites of all time but it is rather smelly to make, so be sure to turn on the extractor fan and open a window (we both smelt like sweet potato dip for the first year of running Good Life until I forced Shirin to take it off the menu, in fear of being single for the rest of my life).

SERVES 8

2 sweet potatoes, peeled and
     roughly chopped into cubes
45ml olive oil
1 tsp ground cumin
15g piece of fresh ginger,
     peeled and grated
1 garlic clove, peeled and very
     finely chopped
½ tbsp white wine vinegar
20g harissa paste
salt

1. Preheat the oven to 200°C/400°F/Gas mark 6 and line a baking tray with parchment paper.

2. Put the chopped sweet potato into a large bowl or container, pour over the olive oil, ground cumin, fresh ginger, garlic, vinegar, harissa paste and a little salt to season. Mix well, then spread the potato out on the lined baking trays and roast in the hot oven for 20 minutes, or until soft.

3. Remove from the oven and put the sweet potato into a large bowl while still warm. Using a potato masher, or the back of a fork, mash everything together. It doesn't have to be perfectly smooth; some texture is a good thing. Check the seasoning, then leave to cool slightly. Serve warm or at room temperature.

> Tip: This is amazing topped with Homemade Dukkah (see page 180) and some crispy flatbreads for dipping.

CARAMELISED ONION HUMMOUS

This is the best snack healthy option of all time. I'm always trying to find variations for hummous and I have to say I think we may have topped it off with this one – FAVE afternoon snack option with carrot sticks.

SERVES 8

1 x 400g tin chickpeas, drained

25g tahini (sesame seed paste)

1 tbsp lemon juice

2 tsp agave nectar or honey

1 garlic clove, peeled

75ml olive oil, plus extra to garnish

salt and freshly ground black pepper

Everything Crackers (see page 201),
   to serve

FOR THE CARAMELISED ONION

2 small red onions, peeled and
   thinly sliced

4 tbsp balsamic vinegar

1 tbsp agave nectar

1 tbsp olive oil

a pinch of salt

freshly ground black pepper

1. For the caramelised onion, toss all the ingredients together in a bowl, then put them into a small saucepan and bring to the boil. Reduce the heat and simmer for 20 minutes, stirring occasionally until the onions are dark and sticky. Allow to cool. Set aside 2 tablespoons of the caramelised onions for garnish.

2. Add all the chickpeas and all the ingredients along with the caramelised onion into a food processor and blitz until completely smooth. Season well with salt and pepper. If it is a little too thick, add a few tablespoons of water.

3. Transfer the hummous to a serving bowl and garnish with the reserved caramelised onion, and a drizzle of olive oil. Serve with Everything Crackers (see page 201) or vegetable crudítes.

SIMPLE CRUDITE DIP

This recipe is super special to us, as it derives from The Ashram, a yoga detox in Spain, where Shirin was proposed to (YEHHHHHHH!). The miso and tahini create such an interesting balance in flavour, which you wouldn't usually expect. It is so YUMMY with a raw summer veggie assortment.

SERVES 2-4

4 tbsp white miso paste

6 tbsp tahini (sesame seed
    paste)

4 tbsp balsamic vinegar

TO SERVE

cauliflower florets
cucumber batons
celery sticks
carrot sticks
any other vegetables
    of your choice

Recipe pictured on this page
and overleaf.

1. Whisk all the ingredients together in a bowl until smooth. Serve with chopped raw cauliflower, cucumber, celery and carrots.

Tip: You can also use this dip as a salad dressing, just add a few tablespoons of water to thin it out. It's delicious on spinach!

HOMEMADE DUKKAH

CRACK DUST! This is what I like to call it, so sprinkle that goodness on everything and anything. Confession; it's bangin' on a grilled cheese sandwich.

MAKES 250G

75g whole, skin-on almonds

75g blanched hazelnuts

25g coriander seeds

30g cumin seeds

55g white sesame seeds

15g nigella (black onion) seeds

1½ tsp sea salt

pinch of cracked black pepper

1. Preheat the oven to 180°C/350°F/Gas mark 4.

2. Using 2 separate baking trays, roast the almonds and hazelnuts on one baking tray for 10–15 minutes until brown, then set aside. Then roast the coriander seeds and cumin seeds for 3–5 minutes. Remove from the oven, without mixing any of them.

3. While the nuts and seeds are both still warm, start by adding the coriander and cumin seeds to a food processor and blitz until smooth, then add in the almonds and hazelnuts and pulse a few times, just enough to lightly crumble them. Add the mixture to a bowl and combine with sesame seeds, nigella seeds, sea salt and black pepper.

4. Transfer the mixture to an airtight container and store for up to 1 month.

> Note: This mixture is delicious sprinkled on any dips and amazing sprinkled on a simple fried egg!

ORANGE AND OMEGA SPRINKLE

You never thought you'd see a breakfast sprinkle, but here it is. My fave is on our quinoa porridge, but you can pretty much sprinkle it on anything SWEET (being the key adjective). I may have sprinkled it on my eggs once, but I would certainly advise against that.

MAKES 340G

40g poppy seeds
40g linseeds (flaxseeds)
40g sunflower seeds
60g white sesame seeds
80g flaked almonds
80g hemp seeds
finely grated zest of 4 oranges

1. Preheat the oven to 180°C/350°F/Gas mark 4.

2. Mix together all the seeds and the zest in a bowl. Spread the mixture out in a single layer on a non-stick baking tray and toast in the hot oven for 15 minutes.

3. Store in an airtight container for up to 3 weeks.

OLIVE TAPENADE

This tapenade is such a flavoursome dip and it is made with classic Mediterranean ingredients. I always find it best to stay true to the natural flavours and ingredients of the region to achieve the best possible taste. Use this in sandwiches or as a dip or, my personal fave, as a topping on fish or poultry!

MAKES 150G

200g pitted black olives,
    preferably Niçoise or Kalamata
3 tbsp capers, well rinsed if
    packed in salt
2 tbsp chopped parsley
1 garlic clove, peeled and
    crushed
finely grated zest of 1
    small lemon
1 tbsp chopped thyme
juice of ½ lemon
5 tbsp extra virgin olive oil
salt and freshly ground black
    pepper (optional)

You will need a food processor.

1. Put the olives into a food processor with the capers, parsley, garlic, lemon zest and thyme, and blitz to a rough purée. Add the lemon juice and, with the motor still running, add the olive oil in a thin steady stream until it is all incorporated and the mixture is a smooth paste. Taste and add more lemon juice and salt and pepper, if necessary.

2. Simply store in an airtight container in the fridge for up to 2 weeks and enjoy with vegetable crudités (see page 176) or as a sandwich spread.

ALMOND PESTO

Best. Pesto. Ever.

MAKES 500G

80g Parmesan, cut into chunks
80g roasted and salted almonds
2 garlic cloves, peeled
200ml olive oil
225g basil, roughly chopped
120g baby spinach
sea salt

You will need a food processor.

1. Put the Parmesan into a bowl with the almonds and garlic and mix together. Remove the mixture and set aside.

2. Depending on the size of your food processor, you will need to do this in parts to avoid over crowding the machine. Add equal parts of all the ingredients into the food processor by adding some of the Parmesan mixture, some of the olive oil, a handful of basil and a handful of spinach and blitz until crumbly. You don't want a smooth purée. Scrape out into a large bowl and repeat this process until everything is used up.

3. Store in a sterilised glass jar (see page 36) in the fridge for up to 2 weeks.

SAFFRON YOGURT

Saffron truly is the essence of Persia. I am pretty sure I have waffled on enough about saffron in this book, so I'm going to keep this one short. Meat, eggs, rice... IT JUST WORKS!

SERVES 6-8

2 small pinches of saffron
    threads (about 10 threads)
2 tbsp hot water
250g natural Greek yogurt
1 garlic clove, peeled and
    crushed
1 tbsp lemon juice
2 tsp salt
50ml olive oil

1. In a small bowl, soak the saffron threads in the 2 tablespoons of hot water for 10 minutes.

2. In a separate bowl, combine the yogurt, garlic, lemon juice, salt and the infused saffron water. Slowly whisk in the olive oil, which will thicken the mixture. Cover and leave to chill in the fridge for 1 hour before using, to allow the saffron to infuse into the mixture. The mixture should be the consistency of a hollandaise; if it is too thick, add a splash of water to loosen.

> **Tip:** Don't whisk the mixture in the blender or it will break down the yogurt and the mixture will become too watery.
>
> **Note:** We strongly encourage using natural Greek yogurt, which doesn't contain any gelatine or gums.

SPINACH CASHEW CREMA

LA PIECE de RESISTANCE. The amount of people who have asked us for this recipe ever since we opened is beyond belief, so, finally, here you go! This is particularly good with eggs, fish, meat and veggies.

SERVES 4

100g cashew nuts
5 spring onions, roughly
    chopped
3 tbsp olive oil, plus extra
    for drizzling
1½ tsp nutritional yeast flakes
250ml water
10g basil, stems and leaves
5g tarragon leaves
40g baby spinach
½ tbsp lemon juice
salt and freshly ground black
    pepper

You will need a blender.

1. Soak the cashew nuts in a bowl of boiling water for at least 1 hour, or overnight. Drain before use.

2. Preheat the oven to 180°C/350°F/Gas mark 4.

3. Put the spring onions on a small roasting tray, drizzle with 1 tablespoon of the olive oil and roast in the hot oven for 15 minutes, they should have some colour but you do not want to let them burn. Remove from the oven and roughly chop.

4. Put all the ingredients into a blender, including the soaked cashews and roasted spring onions, and blend for at least 3 minutes until completely smooth. You might have to stop and start the blender a few times and move around the contents. Set aside until needed.

AVOCADO BUTTER

The name says it all. You can use this either as a spread or just as a dip. Imagine guacamole but totally smooth in texture. MmmmMmMmm!

SERVES 4

2 ripe avocados, peeled and stoned

100ml extra virgin olive oil

1 tbsp lime juice

sea salt

3 tbsp water

10g coriander, roughly chopped

You will need a food processor.

1. Put all the ingredients into a food processor and blitz until completely smooth. Use immediately to prevent any browning of the avocado.

CUCUMBER YOGURT

In Iran we call this **Mast-O-Khiar**, and it's one of those things we serve at home with pretty much everything. It can be used as a dip with our **EVERYTHING CRACKERS** (see page 201) or crudités, but my all-time favourite is to have it on the side with rice and our Saffron chicken skewers (see page 143) – a spoonful of heaven should look something like, a bit of rice, a bit of chicken and a bit of that cucumber yogurt... **YOU FEEL ME?**

SERVES 4

60g cucumber

200g coconut or Greek yogurt

1 tsp dried mint

1 tsp salt

1. Finely chop the cucumber into very small pieces.

2. Mix the chopped cucumber with the remaining ingredients in a bowl and set aside until needed.

SHALLOT DRESSING

I've always found it difficult to experiment with salad dressings, as I genuinely believe people tend to be less adventurous at home and stick to the same old salad dressing that they are comfortable with. I absolutely adore the sweetness of shallots and really think this is a **GREAT** one to change things up a little. It's also super-easy to make, too!

SERVES 4-6

45g banana shallots,
   roughly chopped
75ml red wine vinegar
4 tsp wholegrain mustard
200ml extra virgin olive oil,
   or to taste
salt and freshly ground black
   pepper

You will need a blender.

1. Blend the shallots and half the vinegar in a food processor until smooth.

2. Put the shallot and vinegar mixture into a small saucepan with the remaining vinegar and bring to the boil, then reduce the heat and simmer for 5 minutes. Remove from the heat and allow to cool in the fridge for 20 minutes.

3. Once cool, add the mustard then whisk in the extra virgin olive oil until it is emulsified. Season with salt and pepper and set aside.

LEMON SAGE VINAIGRETTE

Sage has quite a depth of flavour, so it is best paired with roasted vegetables to keep that kind of earthy flavour profile going throughout the dish.

SERVES 4

75ml lemon juice (about
    2 lemons)
200ml olive oil
8 sage leaves, finely chopped
salt and freshly ground black
    pepper

You can use a blender or
    food processor.

1. Blitz all the ingredients in a high-speed blender or food processor for 2–3 minutes until the dressing is opaque and quite thick. If you don't have a blender, finely chop the sage and whisk your dressing really well until it has a 'whipped' consistency. Season and use to dress your salad.

DIJON VINAIGRETTE

The honey is the star of this recipe. It is the easiest dressing of all time and goes well with literally anything.

25ml Dijon mustard
25ml grainy mustard
25ml honey
100ml white wine vinegar
400ml olive oil

Whisk the mustards, honey and white wine vinegar together in a bowl until well combined. Add a few drops of olive oil and whisk to create an emulsion. The mixture should start to feel thicker. While whisking constantly, slowly drizzle in the olive oil and continue whisking until the mixture thickens.

Store in an airtight container in the refrigerator for up to 2 weeks.

> Whisk well so that the oil doesn't separate from the acid (vinegar) when it reaches the emulsion stage.

TEXAS-STYLE 'RANCH' DRESSING

Homemade ranch dressing is totally the answer, as you can avoid all those added ingredients in shop-bought dressings that I can't even pronounce or don't even know what they are. Once again, it's all about the **CASHEWS** creating the rich creamy texture without any use of heavy dairy products. Serve this dressing with any crunchy salad or with our Baked Chicken Dippaz (see page 58), or as a dip for any of our falafels or burgers.

MAKES ABOUT 400ML

100g raw cashew nuts
6 spring onions, trimmed
2 garlic cloves, peeled
½ tbsp olive oil
salt and freshly ground black
    pepper
200ml water
1½ tsp lemon juice
1 tsp onion powder
2 tsp chopped basil
1 tsp chopped parsley

You will need a blender or
    food processor.

1. Soak the cashews in a bowl of boiling water for at least 1 hour.

2. Preheat the oven to 220°C/425°F/Gas mark 7. Line a couple of lightly greased baking trays with parchment paper.

3. Put the spring onions and garlic on the lined baking trays, drizzle with the oil and season with salt and pepper. Roast in the hot oven for 10–15 minutes until blackened and fragrant. Remove from the oven and allow to cool, then rough chop.

4. Drain the cashews and place in a high-speed blender with all the ingredients and blend until completely smooth, adding a little more water if it's too thick.

CHIPOTLE SAUCE

Chipotles are one of my favourite chillies (it's actually a smoked dried jalapeño pepper, which I didn't know until looking it up on the internet right now). This sauce is almost like a spicy, lighter sour cream, and goes really well with everything.

SERVES 2–3

100g cashews
100ml water
15g chipotle in adobo sauce,
    seeds removed
1 tsp lemon juice
1 tsp salt
2 tbsp olive oil

You will need a blender or
    food processor.

1. Soak the cashews in boiling water for at least 1 hour.

2. Drain the cashews. Put all the ingredients into a food processor and blitz until completely smooth. Transfer to a bowl, cover and chill immediately so that it sets before serving.

MUNCHEEZ

BEE POLLEN SNACK

Goodness, Gracious, GREAT BALLS OF BEE POLLEN. Blended dates and sultanas add sweetness to these **AMAZEBALLS** and don't compromise the crunchy texture from the nuts – energising, and the perfect healthy snack to keep you fuelled and pumpin' throughout the day.

MAKES 15 BALLS

150g roasted almonds
50g pecan nuts
150g dried dates
100g sultanas
15g bee pollen

You will need a food processor.

1. Set a large mixing bowl aside as you will be blending all of the ingredients separately.

2. Put the almonds and pecans in a food processor and blitz until chunky, then place in a bowl. Blitz the dates and sultanas, and as soon as they are crumbly put them in the bowl. You don't want to blend them into a paste.

3. Add the bee pollen to the bowl and, using clean, damp hands, mix everything together well. Roll the mixture into 30g balls.

Note: Store in an airtight container for 1 month.

APPLE AND CRANBERRY PROTEIN BARS

Shake things up a little with this NO-BAKE recipe. Forget about your boring shop-bought protein bars, you get the tartness from the dried cranberry then, BOOM, the sweetness of the apple cuts right through it, creating what I like to call A MOUTH-GASM.

MAKES 4–5 BARS

210g dried apples
100g dried, unsweetened
   cranberries
50g protein powder
130g hazelnuts
100g almond butter or
   other nut butter
60g popped quinoa
20g whole linseeds
30g desiccated, unsweetened
   coconut

You will need a food processor.

1. Blitz the dried apples, cranberries and protein powder together in a food processor until finely chopped, then remove and set aside.

2. Blitz the hazelnuts until finely crumbled. Add the dried apple mixture back into the food processor along with the nut butter and pulse a few times. You still want texture, but it should just be sticky. Put everything into a large bowl and fold in the popped quinoa, linseeds and desiccated coconut and mix together with your hands.

3. Place the mixture in the middle of a lined baking tray and cover with a piece of parchment paper. Using a rolling pin or wine bottle, roll it out until it is about 4cm thick, or however thick you like your bars to be, and try to shape it as close to a rectangle as possible, using the sides of a knife to push the sides straight. Refrigerate for 1 hour before cutting into bars.

Note: Store in an airtight container and keep in the refrigerator for up to 2 weeks.

EVERYTHING CRACKERS

I love a good cracker loaded with seeds and flavourings. This recipe is very easy and you can basically throw in whatever seeds you have in your cupboard. I have suggested my preferred ingredient combo, but you can play around with it however you like.

SERVES 4–5

150g chestnut flour
100g brown rice flour
2 tbsp sesame seeds
1 tbsp nigella seeds
2 tbsp sunflower seeds
1 tbsp sea salt
100ml water
100ml olive oil

1. Preheat the oven to 180°C/350°F/Gas mark 4. Tear 3 pieces of parchment paper to fit the length of your baking tray. Line the baking tray with one piece of parchment paper.

2. Combine all the dry ingredients together in a large bowl and then slowly pour in the water and olive oil. Mix well with your hands until you can form a ball then divide the dough into 2 even balls.

3. Place one ball in the middle of one of the reserved pieces of parchment paper and cover with the remaining piece of parchment paper. Roll out until the dough is paper thin, about 1cm. Remove the top piece of parchment paper and place the rolled-out dough onto the oven tray. Bake immediately in the hot oven for 15 minutes, or until golden. Slide the baked sheet of cracker, while still on the paper, off the oven tray and leave to cool. Repeat this process with the second ball of dough.

4. Once the pieces have cooled completely, break them into large crackers and eat straight away with any of our dips.

> Note: These can be stored in an airtight container for a week.

BROWNIE
BITES £3.75

EASY CHOCOLATE, BANANA AND QUINOA BREAD

I've always been a sucker for sweet loaves, especially anything banana related, as it reminds me of being a kid. The riper the banana, the better the flavour and the smell in your kitchen will be all worth it, and it's GLUTEN-FREE!

SERVES 6-8

olive oil, for greasing

150g quinoa flour

50g gluten-free oats

1 tsp bicarbonate of soda

1 tsp ground cinnamon

50g dark chocolate chips
    or chunks

1 tbsp chia seeds

3 ripe bananas, peeled

2 tbsp maple syrup or honey

1 egg

150g crunchy almond butter
    (or any nut butter)

120ml almond milk

You will need a food processor
    or blender.

> Note: Feel free to substitute the chocolate chips for any chopped nuts if you don't want to make the bread as indulgent.

1. Preheat the oven to 170°C/325°F/Gas mark 3 and grease an 900g loaf tin with olive oil.

2. Toast the quinoa flour by putting it in a dry frying pan and heating over a low heat for about 10 minutes. This deepens the flavour of the flour and removes the greasiness that quinoa flour can have. Set aside.

3. Blitz the oats in a food processor or blender until it is a floury consistency, then place in a large mixing bowl with the toasted quinoa flour, bicarbonate of soda, cinnamon, chocolate chips and chia seeds and mix together until combined.

4. Put the bananas, maple syrup, egg, almond butter and almond milk in a separate bowl and, using the back of a large fork, mash the bananas until the mixture is fully combined and almost smooth. You will have a few small chunks of banana. Add the banana mixture to the flour mixture and mix well, then pour the cake batter into the prepared loaf tin and smooth the top. Bake on the middle shelf of the oven for 50 minutes, or until it has slightly risen and become golden. Test that the cake is done by inserting a small knife into the middle, if it comes out clean then it's cooked.

5. Turn the loaf out of the tin and leave to cool on a wire rack.

COCOA COCO BOMBS

Bounty, but ball shaped, and no added nasties... NOT TOO SHABBY.

MAKES 8 BOMBS

85g shredded coconut

60g coconut oil, melted

3 tbsp cacao powder

3 tbsp agave nectar or
maple syrup

½ tsp vanilla extract

1 tbsp ground flaxseed

1. Mix all the ingredients together in a bowl and then
   roll into small balls, about 2.5cm in diameter.

2. Place on a tray lined with greaseproof paper
   and transfer to the fridge for 20 minutes to harden.

3. Serve them straight from the fridge.

CRANBERRY SNACK

These, believe it or not, will keep for a month, so make them in batches and snack on through! (Make sure you keep them in an airtight container in the fridge.) You can also make them into bars or little squares rather than balls. I remember my grandma would make a variation of these and serve them as a little treat with afternoon tea or coffee.

MAKES 13–15 BALLS

180g raw cashew nuts
40g goji berries
180g dried cranberries
1 tbsp sumac
1 tbsp dried ground ginger
½ tbsp nutritional yeast flakes
20g golden linseeds (flaxseeds)

You will need a food processor.

1. Using a food processor, blitz the cashews to a fine crumble and set aside.

2. Blitz the remaining ingredients together until they are crumbly. Depending on the size of your food processor, add the cashews back in to the cranberry mixture. If your food processor is small, do it in batches. Remove the mixture, and with clean, damp hands, roll it into golf-sized balls.

Note: Store in an airtight container for 3 weeks.

BAKED CHICKPEA 'NUTS'

A GRAYYYYYTTTTT alternative to your regular salted bag o' nuts, it's like a crunchy bean/nut vibe without the greasiness of regular nuts. It's also an exceptional snack choice if you have nut allergies!

SERVES 3–4

1 x 400g tin chickpeas, drained
   and rinsed
1 tbsp olive oil
1 tsp salt
1 tsp garlic powder
1 tsp paprika

1. Preheat the oven to 180°C/350°F/Gas mark 4.

2. Blot the chickpeas dry with kitchen paper. You want to blot them as dry as possible so they get nice and crunchy, then toss the chickpeas in the olive oil and seasonings.

3. Spread the chickpeas over a non-stick baking tray and bake on the top third of the hot oven for 20–30 minutes, tossing 2–3 times until crispy and golden. Leave to cool before serving.

> Note: Store in an airtight container for 1 week.
>
> Variation: Use any flavouring you like – curry powder or cumin, or add in a tablespoon of soy sauce for extra zing.

CARROT AND CUMIN CRISPS

Cumin and carrot create a sweet, warm flavour combo combined with the crunch of roasting, it reminds me of a brisk autumn day in Tehran. PERFECTION ALERT: on the kids' snack radar.

3 carrots (about 300g), the
    fatter the better, peeled
1–½ tbsp olive oil
¾ tsp ground cumin
1 tbsp sea salt
freshly ground black pepper

1. Preheat the oven to 180°C/350°F/Gas mark 4.

2. Using a potato peeler, make ribbons from the carrots, starting from the root end, and place into a bowl. Work your way around the carrot – you may need to apply a little bit of pressure to get a thick even ribbon. Drizzle with the olive oil and ground cumin and toss together to make sure that the ribbons are completely coated.

3. Arrange the carrot ribbons on a non-stick baking sheet in a single layer and season with the salt and pepper to taste. Roast in the hot oven for about 10 minutes, turning the carrots once to make sure they are cooking evenly all over. Once they are light brown and crispy, remove from the oven and blot on kitchen paper to drain off any excess oil.

4. Eat immediately with any of our amazing dips, such as the Caramelised Onion Hummus (see page 174) or our Beetroot Dip (see page 168) or dip straight into natural Greek yogurt.

Store in an airtight container for up to 5 days.

PARSNIP CRISPS

I have to make a confession here: I used to be a crisp addict. I think it was a combination of having a terrible routine at university mixed with teenage laziness, but once Shirin introduced me to the prospect of making your own veggie crisps, it CHANGED EVERYTHING. Quick, easy and just so happens to be good for you... need I say more?

SERVES 4

6 parsnips, peeled
3 tbsp olive oil
1 tbsp garlic granules or powder
sea salt and freshly ground
    black pepper

You will need a mandoline.

1. Preheat the oven to 180°C/350°F/Gas mark 4.

2. Using a mandoline, thinly slice the parsnips, starting from the root end, and place into a bowl. Drizzle with the olive oil and toss together. Add the garlic granules and toss again to make sure that the slices are completely coated.

3. Arrange the parsnip ribbons on a non-stick baking sheet in a single layer and season with sea salt and pepper to taste. Roast in the hot oven for about 10 minutes, turning the parsnips every few minutes to make sure they are cooking evenly all over. Be careful that they don't burn. Once they are light brown and crispy, remove from the oven and blot on kitchen paper to drain off any excess oil. Eat immediately.

Note: Store in an airtight container for 5 days.

BANANA PUDDING

Just the word pudding on its own is an exciting notion for me. **COMBINED WITH BANANA IS KILLING THE GAME.** Before writing this I searched online for banana pudding and I didn't know it had such a heartwarming history, I think I like it even more now. Here's a twist on our all-time favourite classic American pud.

SERVES 3-4

160ml canned coconut cream

1 tbsp vanilla extract

4 tbsp arrowroot powder

4 egg yolks

75g honey

400ml coconut milk

1 banana (about 150g),
    sliced into thin rounds

2 tbsp coconut oil

2 tbsp xylitol

Note: Make sure that you buy a good-quality coconut milk.

Tip: Don't let the coconut milk or the pudding mixture boil at any point or it will form an undesirable thick skin. Cover with clingfilm before placing in the fridge to stop the skin from forming.

---

1. Chill the coconut cream in the fridge for at least 2 hours until it is completely chilled and it has become solid.

2. In a bowl, combine half of the vanilla with arrowroot powder, egg yolks and honey and set aside.

3. Warm the coconut milk (not cream!) gently in a pan, you don't want it to boil, then slowly pour it into the egg mixture while stirring well. Once you have poured all the coconut milk into the egg mixture, pour back into the pan and continue to whisk over a medium–low heat until thick. Do not let the mixture boil or spit. Transfer to a bowl or dish, add in the banana slices (leaving a few slices for garnishing), cover with clingfilm and chill until cooled.

4. Meanwhile, make the whipped coconut cream. Whip the chilled coconut cream, coconut oil, xylitol and the ½ tablespoon vanilla together in a large bowl with an electric hand mixer until it is light and fluffy. If you don't have a hand mixer, use a whisk.

5. Once the pudding is cooled, spread the whipped coconut cream over the top of the banana layer and garnish with a few banana slices. If you want the cream to be firmer, cover with clingfilm and allow to set for an hour before serving.

GLUTEN-FREE CHOCOLATE CHIP COOKIES

As much as people associate the term gluten-free with something that has a similar consistency to an old leather shoe, I can safely say that it is not the case with this recipe. If the Cookie Monster was real, it would be ME, so take my word for it – **CHEWY, OOEY, GOOEY** love in the mouth!

MAKES 10-12 COOKIES

2 eggs
100g coconut oil, melted
100g coconut sugar
80g maple syrup
2 tsp vanilla paste
100g gluten-free oats,
    blitzed into a flour
90g gram flour
1 tsp bicarbonate of soda
½ tsp baking powder
175g dark chocolate chips
1 tsp sea salt

1. Preheat the oven to 175°C/347°F/Gas mark 4 and line a baking tray with parchment paper.

2. Combine the eggs, melted coconut oil, coconut sugar, maple syrup and vanilla paste in a bowl and whisk well by hand.

3. In another bowl, combine the oats, gram flour, bicarbonate of soda, baking powder, chocolate chips and sea salt. Add the dry ingredients to the wet ingredients and combine well. Scoop the batter into 10–12 small balls and lightly flatten with fingers onto two lined baking trays.

4. Bake in the hot oven for 10 minutes, then rotate the tray for an even bake and bake for 5 more minutes. Remove from the oven and leave to cool on the tray. Enjoy with a glass of Cacao Hazelnut 'Nutella' Milk (see page 246).

BEST CHOCOLATE FUDGE CAKE EVER

I mean, the title pretty much says it all; rich and aromatic beyond belief. For all y'all chocolate lovers out there I would deffo get on it. I was rather sceptical when we started playing around with the courgette element but it really makes the consistency that much FUDGIERRRRRR!

SERVES 8

250g dark chocolate,
   70% cocoa solids
225g courgettes, trimmed
4 large eggs
40g stevia or 80g unrefined
   cane sugar
20g cacao powder
30g cornflour
1 tbsp vanilla extract
pinch of salt

You will need a box grater.

1. Preheat the oven to 180°C/350°F/Gas mark 4. Lightly grease a 20cm round cake tin.

2. Melt 175g of the chocolate in a glass bowl over a pan of boiling water, ensuring the water does not touch the bottom of the bowl.

3. Wash and dry the courgettes and grate very finely. If you don't have a fine grater you can blitz the courgette in a food processor until it's completely mushy. You need 200g of the grated courgette.

4. Separate the egg yolks and egg whites into two clean and dry bowls. Combine the yolks with the stevia or sugar, cacao powder, cornflour, vanilla, grated courgette and the melted chocolate. Stir well until completely combined. Set the bowl aside.

5. In a completely clean and dry bowl, beat the egg whites and a pinch of salt together using a balloon whisk until soft peaks form. You know you have soft peaks when you lift the whisk into the air and the egg white holds its shape.

6. A spoonful at a time, add the egg whites into the chocolate mixture and lightly fold. You want to gently combine so that you can no longer see lumps of egg white.

7. Pour into the prepared cake tin and bake for 25 minutes. Put a skewer or a fork through the middle to check for doneness, the skewer should come out clean.

8. Allow the cake to cool.

9. Melt the remaining 75g of chocolate, again over a pan of simmering water. With a spatula or spoon cover the top of cake with the melted chocolate glaze and allow it to harden before serving.

SIMPLE CHOCOLATE COCONUT LOAF CAKE

So easy and foolproof, it's almost impossible to mess up this loaf cake. I can reassure you on this as my baking skills are below par and something usually goes wrong... You can play around with the cake mixture if you're not feeling the loaf vibe – you can make it into a layer cake or even muffins or cupcakes. LET'S GET BAKIN'!

SERVES 6-8

150g desiccated coconut

70g cacao powder

1 tbsp baking powder

1 large banana (about 125g), peeled

3 eggs

80ml olive oil

125g fresh raspberries (optional)

TO SERVE (optional)

fresh raspberries

coconut yogurt

You will need a food processor.

1. Preheat the oven to 180°C/350°F/Gas mark 4. Line a 900g loaf tin with parchment paper.

2. Put all the dry ingredients in a large bowl and mix together until combined. Set aside.

3. Purée the banana in a food processor until it is completely smooth and gloopy. Add the eggs and olive oil and whizz until completely combined, then pour the mixture into the dry ingredients and stir well. Pour the batter into the lined loaf tin, top with the raspberries (if using) and lightly press them down into the batter.

4. Bake on the middle shelf of the hot oven for 30 minutes. Different ovens vary, so insert a fork into the middle and if there isn't any mixture clinging to the tines when you remove it then the cake is cooked. Turn out of the tin and leave to cool on a wire rack.

5. Serve with fresh raspberries and a spoonful of coconut yogurt or enjoy plain.

> Note: This mixture can also be made into a layered cake or muffins.

CARAMELISED BANANAS

I am sure you are now aware of our banana obsession, so this is best served with a scoop of coconut yogurt or even vanilla ice cream. I kinda want some right now…

SERVES 4

2 large bananas

3 tbsp honey or natural liquid sweetener

1 tbsp water

1 tsp vanilla extract

½ tsp ground cinnamon

2 tbsp flaked almonds

1 tbsp coconut oil

4 tbsp coconut yogurt or Greek yogurt, to serve

1. Peel the bananas, cut in half horizontally and then cut in half again to make 4 pieces from each banana.

2. In a bowl, combine the honey, water, vanilla and cinnamon, then add the banana slices and mix to coat the bananas.

3. Warm a non-stick pan over a medium heat, add the flaked almonds and toast for 3–4 minutes until golden. Remove from the pan and set aside.

4. In the same pan, add the coconut oil and let melt over a medium heat. Add the bananas, then increase the heat to high and cook for 5–7 minutes until the banana slices are golden and caramelised.

5. Divide the caramelised bananas among 4 serving plates, decorate with the toasted almonds and serve with a spoonful of yogurt.

PECAN RASPBERRY LAYER BAR

This is a favourite dessert bar. Pecan and raspberry go beautifully together but the real secret component that makes this so wonderfully indulgent is the combination of the cashew coconut cream and raspberries. YUM!

SERVES 5–6

FOR THE BASE

100g pecan nuts
1½ tbsp maple syrup
¼ tsp salt
¼ tsp ground cinnamon
60g dried apricots
1 tbsp coconut oil, melted

FOR THE FILLING

150g raw cashew nuts
200ml coconut milk
2 tbsp coconut oil
¼ tsp salt
15g xylitol
70g fresh raspberries

FOR THE TOPPING

30g desiccated coconut
100g fresh raspberries, cut
    into pieces
12 whole pecan nuts

You will need a food processor or
    high-speed blender.

1. Preheat the oven to 180°C/350°F/Gas mark 4. Line the base of a 20cm square springform cake tin with parchment paper.

2. For the filling, soak the cashews in a bowl of boiling water for at least 1 hour, until soft.

3. Meanwhile, for the base, put the pecans in a bowl, add the maple syrup, salt and cinnamon and mix until the nuts are coated. Spread out the pecans on a non-stick baking tray and toast them on the middle shelf of the hot oven for 10–15 minutes until golden. Keep an eye on them as they can easily burn. Remove and leave to cool before using.

4. Once the pecans are cool, blitz them with the dried apricots and coconut oil in a food processor to form a crumbly texture. Pour the mixture into the lined tin and push it over the base and into the sides, making sure it is compact and evenly spread across the bottom. Freeze while you make the filling.

5. Drain the cashews and place in a food processor or high-speed blender with the coconut milk, coconut oil, salt and xylitol and process until the mixture is completely smooth. Add the raspberries and pulse 2–3 times. Do not blend. You should have chunks of raspberry, it shouldn't be solid pink.

6. Remove the base from the freezer and pour the cashew and raspberry mixture over the top. Sprinkle with the desiccated coconut and raspberry pieces and freeze for 2–3 hours until set. Decorate with the whole pecans, slice and serve.

PEANUT BUTTER AND BANANA COOKIES

Oh Hiiiiiiii! It's the cookie monster again, saying helllloooooo. I don't really need to say anything more than PEANUT BUTTER AND BANANA to be honest with y'all. Oh, and it's gluten-free!

MAKES 12–14 COOKIES

150g gluten-free oats

50g coconut palm sugar or soft
   brown sugar

1 tsp baking powder

1/4 tsp salt

1/4 tsp bicarbonate of soda

150g ripe banana (about 1 banana)

60ml coconut oil

80g peanut butter

1 tbsp vanilla extract

You will need a food processor.

1. Preheat the oven to 150°C/300°F/Gas mark 2.

2. Start by blitzing 50g of the oats into a flour in a food processor. Put into a large bowl and combine well with the remaining oats, sugar, baking powder, salt and bicarbonate of soda. You don't need to clean out the food processor.

3. Add the bananas to the food processor and blitz until smooth, then add the coconut oil, peanut butter and vanilla extract and pulse to combine. Add the banana mixture to the dry ingredients and mix well until it forms a dough. Roll the dough out into 12–14 balls and then flatten the balls with 2 fingers. Arrange on a non-stick baking tray, with a little space left inbetween as they spread during baking. Bake in the hot oven for 15 minutes, or until golden.

4. Remove from the oven, transfer to a wire rack and allow to cool.

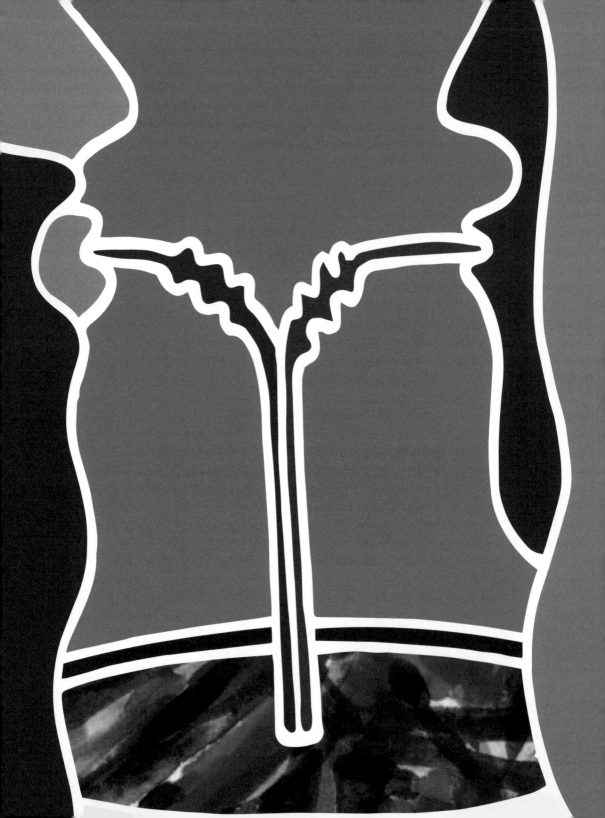

SMOOTHIES AND DRINKS

SMOOZIEEE WOOOZIE WOOOOOOOO! Smoothies are deffo THE MEAL REPLACEMENT of the century. In a rush? Don't have time to prepare a meal and sit down to eat it? Smoothies are the answers to your prayers. Not only do the nutrients get absorbed into your bloodstream quickly, the residual fibres from the blending process aids digestion in more ways than you can imagine.

KIDS AND BABIES LOVE ME! I'm not joking, the amount of goodness in each of the following recipes are ideal for kids and babies. I still have a nine-year-old's taste when it comes to certain things, so this is the ideal way of getting 'younguns' to have their five-a-day along with any other important nutrients they need, without it being YUCKY or EWWWWW. I remember my mum trying to feed my brother and I greens and fruits, poor woman!

SUSTAINABILITY IS KEY – they are a great way to reduce food waste at home, you can usually clear out your fridge by using any excess fruits and veg and rummage through your storecupboard for any nuts, dried fruit, superfoods, etc. – all by making a smoothie!

PROTEIN POWDER – In our stores we tend to market our smoothies as being a pre-/post-gym pick-me-ups. The majority of the time our customers will add protein to their smoothies, sometimes even up to 30g, but this is optional. There are so many different proteins available, ranging from whey, pea, hemp, etc., with various flavourings. My only advice would be to try to find one that has the most natural ingredients, with no synthetic flavourings, and one that fits your dietary requirements.

MALIBU SUNRISE

Feel the wind in your hair, cruisin' down the Pacific coast highway in your convertible, sun shining, sippin' on this bad boy. ARE YOU FEELING MY CURRENT VIBE? I think so.

MAKES 1 LARGE SMOOTHIE

110g strawberries, washed

250ml coconut milk

juice of ½ lime

1 ripe banana, peeled and
    roughly chopped

1 serving of vegan or whey
    protein powder (optional)

4 ice cubes

1 tbsp goji berries, to serve

You will need a Vitamix or
    blender.

1. Put all the ingredients, except the goji berries, into a Vitamix or blender and blend until smooth. Pour into a glass, top with the goji berries and serve.

COCOBUTTER

Coconut and peanut butter is pretty much the DREAM TEAM of (good) life. I really like to add a handful of granola to this one, and have it for breakfast – currently drooling, while writing.

MAKES 1 LARGE SMOOTHIE

1 banana

250ml coconut milk

1½ tbsp peanut butter

2–3 pitted dates, torn into pieces

1 tsp vanilla paste

4 ice cubes

½ tbsp maca powder

1 serving of vegan or whey
    protein powder (optional)

1 tbsp coconut flakes, to serve

You will need a Vitamix or
    blender.

1. Put all the ingredients, except the coconut flakes, in a Vitamix or blender and blend until smooth. Pour into a glass and top with the coconut flakes. Serve.

NINJA TURTLE

This is our **BESTSELLING LOW-SUGAR** smoothie concoction of life! It is extremely subtle on the green-juice flavour spectrum, yet you're still getting all of those juicy nutrients from the great variety of green veg. And it gives you extraordinary turtle ninja powerzzz, I promise!

MAKES 1 LARGE SMOOTHIE

1 handful of baby spinach

½ avocado

¼ English cucumber, chopped

½ tbsp vanilla paste

250ml almond milk (unsweetened or sweetened)

½ tsp spirulina

4 ice cubes

1 serving vegan or whey protein powder (optional)

½ tbsp shelled hemp seeds, to serve

You will need a Vitamix or blender.

1. Put all the ingredients, except the hemp seeds, into a Vitamix or blender and blend until smooth. Pour into a large glass and top with the hemp seeds, then serve.

DOCTOR NOT SO STRANGE

(AKA pear, banana and parsley smoothie.) STOP raising your eyebrows at me! It's not so strange, because adding parsley – or any herb for that matter – to a smoothie should not be approached with caution. Not only do herbs add subtle hints of flavour to smoothies, but they also have important nutritional attributes, ones that you wouldn't normally receive from drinking a solely fruit-based smoothie.

MAKES 1 LARGE SMOOTHIE

1 ripe banana, peeled and
    chopped
1 small pear, chopped
¼ medium avocado, peeled,
    stoned and cubed
10g parsley, leaves and stems
½ tsp spirulina powder
250ml Hemp Milk (see page
    35) or almond milk
4 ice cubes
1 serving of vegan or whey
    protein powder (optional)
1 tbsp hemp seeds, to serve

You will need a Vitamix or
    blender.

1. Put all the ingredients, except the hemp seeds, in a
   Vitamix or blender and blend until smooth. Pour into
   a glass, top with the hemp seeds and serve.

THE BEAR

The ultimate pre- or post-gym smoothie! Wake 'em up with one of these every morning and I'm pretty sure he or she will love you forever. (I've tried it and it worked.) This smoothie is a true example of sheer awesomeness, and who doesn't like that hint of **PEANUT BUTTER** peering through? If you don't like peanut butter, or if you're allergic, use a handful of almonds or almond butter, if you can get a hold of some, instead.

MAKES I LARGE SMOOTHIE

1 handful of baby spinach

1 handful of kale, including
    the stalks

1 tbsp no-added-sugar
    peanut butter

250ml almond milk (unsweetened
    or sweetened)

½ ripe banana, peeled and
    roughly chopped

½ avocado, peeled, stoned
    and chopped

1 tsp vanilla paste

½ tsp spirulina

1 serving of vegan or whey
    protein powder (optional)

4 ice cubes

You will need a Vitamix or
    blender.

1. Put all the ingredients in a blender or Vitamix and blend until smooth. Pour into a glass and serve immediately.

CHOC NORRIS

Probably my favourite chocolate smoothie of all time, with no naughties whatsoever! The avocado might look a bit out of place, combination-wise, but I guarantee you can't even taste it, or notice that it's there. In fact, it gives the drink an extremely creamy texture, creating that rich thickness you expect in a smoothie. The sprinkle of flaked almonds gives it that little extra crunch with every gulp!

MAKES 1 LARGE SMOOTHIE

250ml almond milk

½ banana

½ medium avocado, peeled
and chopped

1½ tbsp raw cacao powder

½ tbsp maca powder

1 tbsp honey or natural
sweetener of choice

1 serving of vegan or whey
protein powder (optional)

4 ice cubes

½ tbsp flaked almonds, to serve

You will need a Vitamix or
blender.

1. Put all the ingredients, except for the flaked almonds, into a Vitamix or blender and blitz until smooth. Pour the liquid into a glass, sprinkle the flaked almonds on top and then serve.

THE HULK

The ingredients combo looks a bit daunting, huh? We have a weird obsessive following at the eateries with this one. I have tried to take it off the menu several times (my own selfish endeavour) but it has always ended in a revolt with our manager frantically calling us with customer complaints. In simpler terms this one is kind of like Marmite. YOU EITHER LOVE IT OR HATE IT!

MAKES 1 LARGE SMOOTHIE

350ml coconut milk

150g pineapple chunks, fresh
    or frozen

1 ripe banana, peeled and
    roughly chopped

4 basil leaves

1 tsp vanilla paste

½ tsp spirulina

4 ice cubes

2 tbsp honey (optional)

1 serving of vegan or whey
    protein powder (optional)

½ tbsp bee pollen, to serve

You will need a Vitamix or blender.

1. Put all the ingredients, except the bee pollen, in the Vitamix or blender and blend until smooth. Pour into a glass, top with the bee pollen and serve.

BERRY GOOD

This one is for all y'all berry lovers out there. I have to admit I have a mild berry phobia, and I still haven't decided if it's the texture or perhaps a childhood trauma, but I'm ready to put any juvenile confusion aside for this bad boy. First of all, the consistency once blended is so super-smooth, it reminds me of the soft-serve ice cream from my youth. Secondly, have you seen those ingredients? Jam-packed full of goodness!

MAKES 1 LARGE SMOOTHIE

50g blueberries
50g blackberries
1 large or 1½ small bananas
2 tbsp almond butter
2 tbsp honey
250ml almond milk or rice milk
4–6 ice cubes
1 serving of vegan or whey
    protein powder (optional)
1 tbsp Gluten-free Granola
    (see page 29), to garnish

You will need a Vitamix or
    blender.

1. Put all the ingredients into a Vitamix or blender and blend until smooth. Pour into a glass and top with the Granola. Serve.

CACAO HAZELNUT 'NUTELLA' MILK

I mean... whoever doesn't like chocolate milk doesn't like puppies or sunshine.

MAKES 2 LITRES

500g roasted hazelnuts

2 litres water, plus extra
    for soaking

4 tsp vanilla bean paste

4 tbsp maple syrup

30g cacao powder

1 rounded tbsp coconut oil,
    melted

pinch of sea salt

You will need a blender or food
    processor and a nut-milk bag
    or muslin cloth.

1. In a bowl, soak the hazelnuts in enough water to cover for 3–4 hours or overnight, then drain and discard the water.

2. In a high-speed blender, combine the soaked hazelnuts with the 2 litres of water and the remaining ingredients and blend until completely smooth.

3. Strain the liquid through a nut-milk bag into a wide bowl, then pour into a large sterilised bottle or jam jars and store in the fridge for up to 3 days.

MATCHA COOLER

If you're not familiar with matcha, please use your trusty everyday tool – the internet, to become so immediately, **BECAUSE YOU'RE MISSING OUT!** It's all the rage in Japan and there is a reason why... it tastes amazing and it just so happens to be good for you. No wonder the Japanese have some of the highest life expectancies in the world! This cooler is the perfect summer non-alcoholic party punch (you can always add some vodka if you're feeling naughty).

SERVES 4

450ml fresh orange juice (about
    6–7 oranges)
200ml fresh lemon juice (about
    5–6 lemons)
1 tbsp matcha powder
2 tbsp water
lots of ice cubes
slices of orange, to garnish

You can use a juicer, or
    squeeze the fruit by hand.

1   Pour the orange and lemon juice into a large
    glass jug.

2   In a separate cup, stir the matcha powder and water
    together vigorously with a fork or a small whisk until
    the matcha has completely dissolved in the water. If
    you don't do this step you could risk having clumps of
    matcha, and no one will want that!

3   Pour the matcha mixture into the orange and lemon
    juice and stir well. Add ice to your cups and pour
    the matcha cooler over. Garnish with an orange
    slice and enjoy!

INDEX

To our Families, thank you for your unconditional love and support. We wouldn't have been able to do this without you.

To our Team, our gratitude goes beyond anything we could put into words.

And to our other halves, thank you for putting up with us throughout it all.

ACKNOWLEDGEMENTS

WELCOME TO THE GOOD LIFE